THE WORKS
OF
ROBERT FERGUSSON

THE WORKS

OF

ROBERT FERGUSSON

JAMES THIN

1970

THE MERCAT PRESS : EDINBURGH

This is facsimile of the 1807 edition of Fergusson's works. 750 copies have been printed, and the first ten of these bound specially in full morocco.

469

Published by

JAMES THIN, Bookseller, SOUTH BRIDGE
EDINBURGH

Printed by Unwin Brothers Ltd.
The Gresham Press, Old Woking, Surrey, England
A Member of the Staples Printing Group

Ogburn sculp.

ROBERT FERGUSSON.

Published for Oddy & C.º May 1807.

THE

WORKS

OF

ROBERT FERGUSSON.

TO WHICH IS PREFIXED, A

Sketch

OF THE

AUTHOR'S LIFE.

———————

LONDON:

PRINTED FOR S. A. & H. ODDY, 27, OXFORD STREET.

....

1807.

Oliver & Co. Printers, Edinburgh.

CONTENTS.

4

SCOTS POEMS.

6

PREFACE.

The Poems of Robert Fergusson have generally appeared in the most common style of printing. The present edition is offered to the public, as the first effort that has been made to do typographic justice to the excellence of his genius,—an excellence, which Burns, his more celebrated competitor for fame, perceived with delight, and praised with ingenuous magnanimity,—an excellence, which he unquestionably out-shone, but on which he gazed with a feeling of inferiority, " to kindle at the blaze." If the publishers, by their humble exertions, shall be able, in any degree, to secure for the Works of Fergusson a place in the libraries of those who are distinguished in society and literature, they will regard their attempt with much satisfaction.

A Sketch of the Poet's Life is prefixed to this edition of his works. The writer of that Sketch was seduced to undertake the task by a strong feeling of indignation. He had read the different and contradictory accounts of Fergusson's

life with a deep interest : and while he made some private
inquiries in consequence of the discrepancies thus presented
to his view, he was led to think, that the public were egre-
giously deceived with regard to some important features in
the character of Fergusson, which had been abominably dis-
torted. The following biographical Sketch was the result :
—it is but a Sketch, faint and imperfect : and the only apo-
logy that is offered for the production of it, is the fact, that no
genuine picture of the character of Fergusson seemed likely
to appear. It was originally intended for a periodical publi-
cation, in which a part of it was printed a few years ago ;
but that work having been relinquished ere the whole was
published, the manuscript was laid aside until it was wanted
as an appendage to the present edition of the Poems. It has
been corrected considerably since it was written; but still it
requires amendment and much indulgence.

Some readers of taste may be dissatisfied with the compo-
sition of the Life : it is hoped, however, they will not con-
sider a juvenile error as inexpiable. It will be some atone-
ment for the present fault, if the sinner cease in future to
present his thoughts to the public eye ; and if he knows his
own purposes, he thinks this is the last time he will ever

expose himself to the condemnation of criticism. To that condemnation, should it be his fate, he will silently submit. He is placed in a situation of life where it can only produce a momentary uneasiness, and where he is required by duty to exile from his bosom all the hopes that can be inspired by literary ambition. He therefore withholds his name from this publication ; not, however, without considering himself bound, when rationally required, to support, by personal responsibility, his assertions in point of fact, or should his reflections of a moral nature be challenged, to welcome any consequences that can follow the public avowal of his name.

If any individual shall conceive himself injured by the language that is used in some of the following pages, (and one person, it is perhaps to be regretted, will be in this predicament), the writer of this is ready to give all expedient redress. But he is not afraid to speak his mind freely and decidedly. He admires that urbanity which is the characteristic of a gentleman; but he despises the sneaking dissimulation of real opinion, which is masked in the guise of politeness, or seeks shelter for its weakness in seeming deference to public prejudices. He thinks that Robert Fergusson's memory, for which he feels an ardent reverence, has been

grossly insulted,—insulted even in the sanctuary of the tomb:
and being of this opinion, he would blush at his own pusil-
lanimity, were he, on the present occasion, to suppress the
utterance of one honest feeling that exists in his heart.

EDINBURGH,
March, 1807.

THE FOLLOWING

SKETCH

OF

THE LIFE OF ROBERT FERGUSSON,

IS INSCRIBED

TO JAMES GRAHAME, ESQ.

AS A TRIBUTE OF

RESPECT FOR HIS WORTH,

AND

ADMIRATION OF HIS GENIUS.

A

SKETCH OF THE LIFE

OF

ROBERT FERGUSSON.

THE errors of genius have often afforded me-
lancholy occasion for the triumphs of prudent
stupidity ; and sometimes they have produced
an affectation of folly and vice, as the appro-
priate marks of mental brightness. Eccentri-
city, and dissipated habits of life, it must be
confessed, have been the frequent concomitants
of high intellectual endowments ; but they are
to be viewed as the mere contingent blemishes,
not as the inseparable associates of genius.

" Angels are bright still, tho' the brightest fell :
" Tho' all things foul would wear the brows of grace,
" Yet grace must still look so."

Vice and profligacy, in the conduct of the
dull and illiterate, pass without observation,

because the beings in whom these deformities
are to be found, grovel in the shades of life,
without exciting interest, or arresting attention.
It must not, however, be supposed, that stu-
pidity, or mediocrity of talent, exempt a man
from the follies and crimes incident to huma-
nity; while, at the same time, there cannot
be a more fatal error than that which sanctifies
imprudence, and neglect of the more rigid
duties of life, by representing such conduct as
the aberrations of a generous spirit. Per-
haps it is possible to derive useful instruction
from exhibiting man as he is always to be
found—an imperfect being: perhaps it is pos-
sible to trace the steps of intellectual pre-emi-
nence through a career of imprudence, without
that imprudence being permitted to assume
the form and complexion of excellence. It is
certainly not impossible to check the shallow
pretensions of affectation, by showing, that the
adventitious dross is not the precious jewel—
that extravagance, thoughtlessness, and ardour
of pursuit, are not the only constituents of
mental superiority.

For a moral picture of this kind, it is diffi-
cult, perhaps, to select a fitter subject than
ROBERT FERGUSSON. His natural talents were
of the highest order; his acquirements were
considerable; and he lived in an age, when

the possession of such qualities, if properly applied, could not have failed to promote his domestic and social comfort. Although, however, he was placed in these circumstances, he never reached the meridian of life. The short period of his existence was distinguished chiefly by its wretchedness; and its close was preceded by madness, the consummation of mortal calamity.

Robert Fergusson was the son of William Fergusson and Elizabeth Forbes. Having served an apprenticeship to a merchant in Aberdeen, William Fergusson came to Edinburgh, in the year 1746, in search of employment. For a considerable time after he resided in Edinburgh, he was occupied as a clerk by people of different descriptions; but latterly he obtained a situation in one of the departments of an extensive mercantile institution *, in which he continued to act as an accountant until the time of his death. He appears to have been an intelligent and respectable man. During the time that he had the management of the affairs of a company of Upholsterers in Edinburgh, he framed a very useful book of rates; and in the earlier part of his life, he indulged himself in the boyish weak-

* The British Linen Company.

ness of writing verses. It is believed, however, that he relinquished this habit when the cares and the duties of manhood banished the day-dreams of youth. He had two sons and two daughters *. Robert, the younger son, was born at Edinburgh, on the 5th of September 1750. During the years of his early infancy, his constitution was so extremely delicate, that his life was frequently despaired of. When six years of age, he was put to an English school, taught by a Mr Philp, in Niddry's Wynd. So considerable was his improvement under Mr Philp, that in half a year he was thought qualified to be initiated in the study of the Latin language, in which he was in-structed by Mr Gilchrist, then one of the masters of the High-school. While in this

* Barbara was married to Mr David Inverarity, cabinet-maker in Edinburgh. Her son, Mr James Inverarity, some years ago, wrote a spirited and elegant critique on Mr Ir-ving's account of his uncle's life, and repelled, with becoming indignation, some very unwarrantable statements made by that gentleman. Margaret was married to Mr Duval, a purser in the Navy. She is an accomplished woman, and possesses a mind that stamps her a genuine relative of Fer-gusson. Harry, the elder brother, was a young man of considerable learning and ingenuity : he chose to atone for some juvenile indiscretions, by entering on board a ship of war : and as his friends have not heard of him for many years, they have no reason to believe he is in life.

seminary, his health was in so precarious a state, that he was frequently obliged to be absent from school. His powers, however, were so active, that even under the disadvantage attending this broken kind of study, he equalled any, and surpassed numbers of his classfellows.

While his school studies were thus interrupted by ill health, he is said to have acquired a taste for books, which he was accustomed to indulge. It is a remarkable fact, that while yet a mere child, his chief delight was in reading the Bible. The Proverbs of Solomon, in particular, attracted his most earnest regard. A curious instance of the effect which this practice produced on his tender and susceptible mind, may be mentioned as a proof of the powerful impression which some circumstances make on the human faculties in the early period of life. One day he entered his mother's chamber in tears, calling to her to whip him. Upon inquiring into the cause of this extraordinary behaviour, he exclaimed, " O mother ! " he that spareth the rod, hateth the child."— The principal object of biography is to gratify curiosity : it may also instruct. From this solitary fact, many interesting inferences may be drawn : but it is less the biographer's business to philosophise than to furnish the materials. The evident connection between the various circumstances of Fergusson's life, and the characteristics of his mind, will be easily traced in the sequel of his story.

After a desultory attendance at the Highschool of Edinburgh, during a period of four years, he went to Dundee, where he studied two years longer. At this time, it seems, his friends had destined him for the church. Accordingly, at the age of thirteen, he entered a student of St Andrews university, where he enjoyed a bursary *, endowed by a Mr Fergusson, to be conferred on persons of the same name. At St Andrews he became conspicuous for the respectability of his classical acquirements, and for those uncommon powers of conversation, which, in his more advanced years, fascinated the associates of his convivial hours. The study of poetry seems also to have attracted his regard, more than the scholastic and mathematical branches of science: for these, indeed, he always expressed the most decided contempt †. It was during his residence at St Andrews, that he first " committed " the sin of rhyme." His juvenile verses were thought to possess considerable merit ; and even the professors, it is said, took particular

* Equivalent to an exhibition in the English universities.

† Irving.—Sommers.

notice of them. It has not been ascertained what was the first object that awakened his fancy, and gave a poetical impulse to his genius: but, it is believed, the first inspirations of his muse were poured forth in satirical castigation of his instructors, and in the commonplace trifles, such as a boy usually writes. The abilities of young Fergusson secured him the regard of Dr Wilkie, author of the Epigoniad, and at that time professor of natural philosophy in the university of St Andrews. He was also patronised by Professor Vilant. It has been said, indeed, that Dr Wilkie occasionally employed Fergusson to read his prelections, when particular circumstances prevented the personal discharge of his duty. This, however, is a very incredible story, and is very satisfactorily explained by Professor Vilant, in a letter to Mr Inverarity on the subject: " A " youthful frolicksome exhibition of your uncle " first directed Dr Wilkie's attention to him, " and he afterwards employed him one sum- " mer, and part of another, if I rightly re- " member, in transcribing a fair copy of his " academical lectures."

The " youthful frolicksome exhibition" alluded to by Professor Vilant, may perhaps be that mentioned by Mr Campbell *, as like-

* " An Introduction to the History of Poetry in Scotland, by Alexander Campbell."

ly to have resulted in Fergusson's academical disgrace. He was a good singer, and on that account was requested oftener than he wished to officiate as precentor at prayers. He resolved to get quit of the drudgery, and adopted a scheme to effect his purpose, which, it is said, excited the displeasure of the different professors against him. It is usual, in Scotch Presbyterian churches, for persons in bad health to ask " the prayers of the congregation." Fergusson, one morning, when in the precentor's desk, rose up with great solemnity, and in the formal style which prevails on these occasions, cried aloud, " Remember in prayer, " —— ——, a young man, (present in the " hall), of whom, from the sudden effects of " inebriety, there appears but small hope of " recovery."

Mr Irving, in the earlier editions of his work, has mentioned, that Fergusson was expelled from the university of St Andrews ; but as some circumstances which followed, of no less importance, are omitted, it is necessary that these should be noticed, even although Mr Irving has in the later editions corrected his faulty statement. The particulars attending this expulsion, are thus detailed in a paper written by Principal Hill, and subscribed by Professor Vilant ; the latter of whom was at the time (January 29th 1801) unable, from sickness, to do more than attest the truth of the account.

" The university of St Andrews keep no re-
" cord of the censures inflicted upon young
" men during the course of their studies, be-
" cause they are willing to hope, that future
" good behaviour will atone for the improprie-
" ties of early days. But as an inquiry has
" been made on the part of the relations of
" Mr Robert Fergusson, whether he was ex-
" pelled from this university, Mr Nicolas
" Vilant, professor of mathematics, the only
" person now in the university who was then
" a member of it, declares, for their satisfac-
" tion, that in the year 1767, as he recollects,
" at the first institution of the prizes given by
" the Earl of Kinnoul, late chancellor of this
" university, there was a meeting, one night
" after the determination of the prizes for that
" year, of the winners, in one room of the
" United College, and a meeting of the losers
" in another room at a small distance ; that in
" consequence of some communication between
" the winners and the losers, a scuffle arose,
" which was reported to the masters of the
" College ; and that Robert Fergusson and
" some others, who had appeared the most
" active, were expelled ; but that the next

" day, or the day thereafter, they were all re-
" ceived back into the College, upon promises
" of good behaviour for the future.

" NICOLAS VILANT."

But young Fergusson's academical career
was not distinguished solely by these kind of
exploits : Others of a more interesting and ho-
nourable kind seemed at least to have been the
objects of contemplation. One, in particular,
which, in my apprehension, throws consider-
able light upon his character and feelings, at
the time, ought here to be mentioned.

It is said by Mr Irving, on the authority of
the Encyclopædia Britannica, where it is stated
as the import of authentic private information,
that Fergusson, during the last year of his
residence at St Andrews, had written two acts
of a tragedy, founded on the story of Sir Wil-
liam Wallace ; but that he relinquished his
plan, from an apprehension that his play might
be deemed a mere copy of some poem which
he had seen on the same subject. There does
not seem to be any satisfactory objection urged
against the truth of this statement* ; and while
it derives probability from the consideration of
other parts of his conduct, and other features

* Sommers' Life, p. 12 and 13.

of his character, it seems to render his claims
to an honourable literary ambition, consider-
ably valid. A few observations on the subject,
although perhaps unnecessary, may not be
deemed superfluous or useless.

It is well known that Fergusson was a rank
Jacobite. Like other Scots poets since his
day*, he sympathised in the sufferings of fallen
greatness. There is something in this passion,
abstracted from every consideration of its pro-
priety in particular cases, so nearly allied to
the generous and the excellent, that it seems
to merit little blame. But, when the spirits of
which it seems (in our days at least), a constitu-
ent part, are examined, it commands our love
and admiration. We sometimes see an enthusi-
astic reverence for those political feelings, by the
influence of which the Stuart family filled, and
would have occupied the British throne, com-
bined with patriotism and an ardent love of li-
berty. There is at least something like it.
We see the poets to whom I allude, at one
time deploring the sinking fortunes of an an-
cient race of monarchs, describing the sorrows
of Charles, or execrating the " merciless
" sword" which scourged the fields of Cul-
loden : at another time, we hear them cele-

* Burns and Campbell.

brating the names of our ancient patriots, or animating their countrymen in the day of danger, to save the liberties of their country. I know not how far this is consistent in a philosophical point of view ; but it is perfectly so in a poetical : for the poet is not expected to reason accurately, but to feel powerfully. That Fergusson participated in this fraternal failing, is extremely probable : for all the prejudices which are apt to adhere to the mind of a youthful and generous Scotsman, were the inmates of his bosom. He regarded the union of his native country with England as a virtual sacrifice of her independence and of her glory ; even liberty itself he seemed to consider as but a phantom, unless it arose from the atchievements of his country's patriots. In an invocation to the River Forth, he thus exclaims :

" On thy green banks sits Liberty enthron'd,
" But not that shadow which the English youth
" So eagerly pursue ; but freedom, bought
" When Caledonia's triumphant sword,
" Taught the proud sons of Anglia to bemoan
" Their fate at Bannockburn, where thousands came,
" Never to tread their native soil again *."

In these circumstances, independent of all direct and positive testimony, there is sufficient

---

* A Saturday's Expedition.

reason for thinking that the story of Sir William Wallace would interest him much; and it is by no means an extravagant supposition, that he might design to delineate our hero's fate in a dramatic form. In some respects, indeed, the subject was admirably calculated for him: it was interesting in itself, and unoccupied by any other person. From his earliest infancy, every Scotsman regards the memory of Sir William Wallace, as that of a being who surpassed the common race of mortals in every attribute which elevates the individual above his species. Strength preternatural was the fabled quality of his body; patriotism and courage the unquestioned characteristics of his mind. His adventures, whether fabulous or true, were of the mixed kind, which excite the most lively interest in a story,—now proudly moving on the highest tide of success,—now deeply overwhelmed by misfortune. His fall too was of that tragical cast, which excites every sympathy of our hearts. There is not perhaps a Scotsman, in the middle and lower ranks of life, who has not read, with a holy enthusiasm, the account of our national hero's exploits, as recorded in the barbarous verse of Henry the Minstrel. Yet, from whatever cause it has arisen, it is true, that none of our poets, even to this day, have celebrated, in a strain sufficiently sublime, the atchievements of Wallace, or delineated, with an adequate truth of poesy, the exalted character of the man. Perhaps no poetical talents are capable of giving to Scotsmen a vivid picture of the greatness of their greatest hero ; his name is associated in our minds with every thing that is illustrious. The poet's field of exertion is thought to be fictitious circumstance : but if the story of Wallace's exploits were even divested of what, doubtless, renders them more rich in the means of poetical embellishment, and although the blaze of our patriot's glory were to shine unmingled with the fire of fancy's creation, they are still too brilliant for the eye of a common poet. That Fergusson, in these circumstances, had the courage to think of such a subject for his poetry, is a strong proof of the ambition of his mind and the elevation of his temper. When we consider the positive testimony in the case, and all the circumstances connected with it, we shall scarcely have a ground for with-holding our assent to the supposition of his purpose : and if we grant the probability of his design, we cannot refuse the tribute of respect for his feelings. That he relinquished his purpose, for the reason assigned, seems both probable and honourable. The spirit which could think of celebrating the he-

roism of Wallace, could ill stoop to the base-
ness of literary theft, or even to the meanness
of servile imitation.

After a residence for four years in St An-
drews, (his bursary having expired, and his
father having died two years before), Ro-
bert resigned all thoughts of pursuing the cleri-
cal profession, and returned to his mother's
house in Edinburgh, without any plan of life,
or rational prospect of future occupation. It
has been thought, that a man of liberal educa-
tion, can easily find some employment in which
to engage; and that in the present state of so-
ciety, he need only seek, in order to obtain, an
adequate reward for the application of his ta-
lents. Numerous instances might be produced
to contradict this notion; and, I am not aware,
that any thing better than facts could be stated
to explode a supposition, which misleads many
parents (particularly in Scotland), in the edu-
cation of their families. Fergusson affords one
example, in which the worldly condition, and
the propensities of character, were completely
opposed to each other, by an unfortunate con-
currence of circumstances. He was placed on
the threshold of life, an unfriended boy; with-
out the means of present support, or the pros-
pect of future provision. He had received a
classical education; he had acquired the habits of

intellectual, rather than of bodily exertion; and he cherished with the ardour peculiar to youth and to genius, the sanguine hopes of future eminence What in these circumstances could he do ? The first and the natural feeling which one so situated is apt to entertain, is a confidence in the exertions of those with whom he is connected by the ties of blood. Fergusson had a mother ; but she was a widow—poor—destitute—friendless : She was a proper object of filial reverence ; but his advancement in the world, could not be materially promoted by her exertions.

He had, however, an uncle who lived near Aberdeen, in affluent circumstances, and who, it seems, was also a man of learning. To him Fergusson paid a visit, in expectation, that he would, by his means, obtain some reputable employment. I write the name of that uncle, John Forbes, with a sentiment of indignation, which even the recollection that he is now insensible to reproach cannot extinguish. Mr Forbes at first treated Fergusson with civility—that kind of civility which was expressed by admitting him to his table, and by the complimental cant of ceremonious hospitality. But even this humble kind of friendship, (and humble it must have appeared in the eyes of Robert Fergusson), did not suit the characteristic brutality of his uncle's spirit. Acting upon a principle, not indeed peculiar to himself, he seems to have regarded the accidental evils of misfortune, as the marks of dishonour. Fergusson's exterior appearance, in point of dress, during a stay of a few months in Mr Forbes's house, had become shabby: And for this crime, his generous relative drove him from a house, in which I think, Robert Fergusson would have been an illustrious guest, although clothed in rags. Deeply wounded in his spirit by such unworthy treatment, he retired from the inhospitable dwelling of his uncle, to a petty ale-house in the neighbourhood. In a letter to his uncle from this place, he gave vent to the feelings of his heart, in a strain of reproach, indignation, and independence, worthy of the pride and sensibility of a poet. He had scarcely left his uncle's house, before that personage felt the qualms of compunction: a messenger was dispatched after the exiled Fergusson, with a few shillings to defray his expences on the homeward road. This peace-offering of a sordid worldling, the poor boy was constrained to accept, in order to avoid the more terrible alternatives of begging, or of perishing for want.

After a fatiguing journey on foot from Aberdeen, which he had accomplished under the united tortures of mortification, resentment, and despondency, he reached his mother's house in Edinburgh. His bodily fatigue, and the chagrin arising from disappointed hopes, confined him to bed for several days after his arrival; but he soon recovered from the shock which his feelings had received, and found a temporary alleviation of his sufferings, in writing verses, " On the decay of Friend- " ship," and " Against Repining at Fortune."

He was soon afterwards employed as an assistant in the office of the Commissary-clerk of Edinbnrgh, where he continued during the remainder of his life, with the exception of a few months that he wrote in the Sheriff-clerk's office*. He could not endure the kind of business which frequently occurred in the latter situation, where Fergusson thought the law too often appeared in the aspect of severity. All proceedings against criminals of various denominations, usually commence in the Sheriff's court. Fergusson therefore solicited and obtained re-admission into the situation which he formerly held. It is not known, that he originally left the Commissary-clerk's office, on

---

* Both Mr Irving and Mr Sommers are mistaken in saying, that he continued in the latter office until his death, from the period that he left the commissary-clerk's office.

account of tyrannical treatment from his superiors, as stated by Mr Irving : on the contrary, it is certain, he frequently amused himself with the trifling peevishness in which the deputy, Mr Abercromby, under whom he acted, indulged. This peevishness was in a great measure owing to the valetudinary state of health under which that gentleman long laboured. He had no dislike at Fergusson, and occasionally employed him in his private affairs ; but his fretful disposition did not accord with Fergusson's feelings. He was, however, upon the whole, extremely unlike many others of those business-machines who are every day to be met with—illiterate, but industrious,—mean in their dispositions, yet presumptuous in their manners ; and who having, by these means, advanced themselves to worldly consideration, conceive themselves fully warranted to trample on, and insult their official inferiors.—He was a man of much knowledge in business, and of considerable ability.

As the epoch of Fergusson's life, which is most interesting in itself, and most fraught with useful instruction, commenced at his entry into the Commissary-clerk's office, I shall detail, as minutely as possible, every authentic particular of importance concerning him, which I have been able to obtain.

During the whole of the period which inter-
vened between his return from college and his
death, he continued almost daily to write
verses on passing occurrences and incidental
topics. He was a constant contributer to Rud-
diman's Weekly Magazine, a popular and re-
spectable miscellany of the day. His dislike
and neglect of his employment seems to have
formed a complete contrast to his literary ar-
dour. This fact, of which we are informed
by the concurring testimony of all his associates,
is pretty amply illustrated by the following
anecdote, communicated by a gentleman who
had the best access to know the facts, and
whose veracity and accuracy may be fully re-
lied on.

It was a principal part of Fergusson's duty
to copy out the extracts of deeds and protests
which were recorded in the Commissary-court
books. This business is the most mechanical
that can well be supposed, being merely to
copy the document recorded, with some trif-
ling additions; yet so completely was Fergus-
son's mind engrossed by matters foreign to
his task, that, in the course of one forenoon,
he blundered the same extract two different
times. When he returned to the office in the
evening, he found that the paper had been
much wanted; and after venting a coarse ex-

pression against the person who molested him,
he sat down a third time to the business. He
had not, however, got his copy half finished,
when he cried out to his office companion, that
a thought had just struck him, which he would
instantly put into verse, and carry to Ruddi-
man's Magazine (on the eve of publication),
but that he would instantly return and com-
plete the extract. He immediately scrawled
out " Verses on Mr Thomas Lancashire," and
ran with them to the press. On his return
towards the office, he called at the shop of
Mr Sommers, Print-seller and Glazier, below
the Commissary office, Parliament Square,
where he found the shop-boy reading a poem
on Creation. This circumstance furnished him
with another topic for versifying, and he wrote
a coarse epigram on his friend Sommers *.
These proceedings occupied him about twenty
minutes ; and having thus given vent to the
effervescence of his fancy, he returned quietly
to his drudgery.

This anecdote shows pretty distinctly his
aversion to the settled employment to which
his attention should have been directed, and

* " Tom Sommers is a gloomy man,
    " His soul is dark with sin ;
  " O holy J...s glaze his soul,
    " That light may enter in."

his wayward wanderings of thought, in regions foreign to his more immediate concerns. He very naturally conceived the scanty emoluments resulting from his labour to be an inadequate reward for the exertion of such talents as he was conscious he possessed; but he unreasonably allowed contempt for his business to superinduce inattention to its duties. To copy law papers of any description, is indeed an occupation excessively irksome to any man whose talents are not wholly placed at the points of his fingers; and the pitiful allowance which Fergusson received for his labour, tended very little to render that irksomeness tolerable. To such disadvantages, however, he should have opposed the considerations of necessity and prudence. Some regular occupation he must have followed, and there is none in life unaccompanied with labour and inconvenience of some kind. Fergusson would have been a happier man, if he had aimed at the acquisition of business habits. He might by such means have reached that real independence which, by industry and frugality, is attainable in almost every condition of life, and which in every condition confers the most genuine comfort and dignity. He should have reflected, that merit cannot always be known; that it is in every case dangerous, and often disgraceful, to be the object of popular support in a pecuniary point of view; and that the earnings of honest industry, though scanty, are sweeter to the heart, imbued with the pride of true independence, than the most profuse munificence which can be conferred on venal prostitution.

I will not say that it was improper in Fergusson to cultivate his poetical talents—far otherwise : but it was unwise to permit what ought to have been only his recreations, to supplant his actual duties. His employment was doubtless sufficiently servile : but still attention to it was by no means incompatible with his devotion to the muses, as has been sagely discovered by some of his biographers. Dry and uninteresting as the study of law, and the practical exercise of juridical functions, may appear to those who are unacquainted with the principles of the one, or the habits of the other, I affirm, from observation of the fact, that they have no peculiar and exclusive tendency to extinguish the ardour of genius ; and if it were not foreign to my present purpose, I could easily mention the names of many lawyers, whose minds are distinguished by every quality that appertains to the poetic character. Upon the hypothesis of juridical studies and poetical talent being incompatible, it can-

not, therefore, be supposed, that Fergusson,
although he was certainly not a lawyer, might
not have been at the same time a poet and an
inferior clerk in a law office ; unless, indeed,
it is thought, that in such a situation it was
presumptuous in him to aspire above the me-
chanical drudgery of penmanship. Fortunate-
ly, however, there is yet no aristocracy in the
republic of letters, elevated and supported by
corporation privileges : Chatterton was an at-
torney's hack, Burns a ploughman.

In addition to Fergusson's dislike of his pro-
fession, other circumstances concurred to in-
fluence his character and determine his fate.
The obvious merit of his poems, which were
widely circulated in Ruddiman's Magazine, at-
tracted public notice ; and his company was
courted with avidity by people of almost every
description. He could rank in the number of
his friends, many of the first characters of his
time in Edinburgh. His unassuming manners,
his wit, and his convivial talents, gave pleasure
to all, but chiefly to the young and the gay.
He was ingenuous, affable, manly, and gene-
rous. His conversation was that of a gentle-
man and a scholar ; his wit the spontaneous
and captivating offspring of genius ; his song
was that simple, but powerful melody, which,
as its energies are directed, arouses, or ravish-

es, or subdues. Tavern parties and clubs were the spheres which Fergusson's wit and song too frequently enlivened ; and these destroyers of every respectable principle in human nature, at length undermined his constitution, sullied his respectability, and disordered his reason.

The extent to which his convivial propensities would make him descend, is exemplified in an anecdote given by Mr Sommers.

" Such were his vocal powers, and attach-
" ment to Scots songs, that in the course of his
" convivial frolics, he laid a wager with some
" of his associates, that if they would furnish
" him with a certain number of printed bal-
" lads (no matter what kind), he would under-
" take to dispose of them as a street singer,
" in the course of two hours. The bet was
" laid ; and next evening, being in the month
" of November, a large bundle of ballads were
" procured for him. He wrapped himself in a
" shabby great coat, put on an old scratch
" wig, and in this disguised form, commenced
" his adventure at the Weigh House, head of
" the West Bow. In his going down the
" Lawnmarket, and High Street, he had the
" address to collect great multitudes around
" him, while he amused them with a variety
" of favourite Scots songs, by no means such

" as he had ballads for, and gained the wager,
" by disposing of the whole collection. He
" waited on his companions by eight o'clock
" that evening, and spent with them, in mirth-
" ful glee, the produce of his street adven-
" ture."

At other times again, his humour would
assume a moral cast, and he would make trick
and jocularity in some measure the means of
usefulness. The following particulars were
communicated to me by a gentleman to whom
I am indebted for some valuable information,
relative to the subject of these memoirs. I
shall give my reader the language of my au-
thority :

" Mr Fergusson had a rooted aversion to
" every kind of hypocrisy, especially religious
" hypocrisy. Those who pretended to an ex-
" traordinary outward show of religion, he
" tortured with much severity of ridicule. A-
" mong others of this stamp, he considered
" his landlord as one worthy of his particular
" attention ; and he gave him now and then
" a little seasonable chastisement His landlord
" was a man as religiously attached to his bot-
" tle as to his prayers ; and though almost e-
" very night he was pretty much overcome by
" the first, he never neglected the last. This
" conduct Mr Fergusson could not long ob-

" serve, without giving him some correction.
" One night, when the landlord had called his
" household together, and in a state of com-
" plete intoxication, was proceeding to pray-
" er, Robert took his station in an adjoining
" closet. The landlord had no sooner fallen
" upon his knees, and uttered the words, *O
" Lord, thou art good and gracious!* than Mr Ro-
" bert, from the closet, in a hollow tone of
" voice, re-echoed his words. The landlord
" being much agitated by this secret assistant,
" did not venture to proceed farther, till he
" had fully ascertained his personal safety.
" Having satisfied himself on this point, he
" uttered the next sentence with tremulous
" gravity: it was again re-echoed by the in-
" visible being, in a more dismal tone. From
" these unhallowed responses, the landlord
" terminated his evening devotion, and gave
" orders to his servants to retire and carry
" *awa' the buiks* After composing himself, by
" serious reflection, he recalled his servants,
" and earnestly enquired if Rabbie Fergusson
" was come home? being answered in the af-
" firmative, (for by this time Robert had
" escaped from his concealment), the land-
" lord proceeded to lecture his auditors on
" the impropriety of their past conduct;
" telling them, that he was certain, from

" what had happened that night and other
" forewarnings, there was something wrong,
" and that some awful calamity would be-
" fal the family; warning them of their dan-
" ger, and cautioning them against all loose
" disorderly behaviour in future. Having thus,
" as he imagined, fortified those under his
" care, by his prophetical visitation, his in-
" ward terror, heightened by guilt, suggested
" to him the necessity of consulting his own
" safety, by some salutary advice: and hav-
" ing, on former occasions, had some share of
" Robert's friendly admonitions, he ventured
" to communicate to him the events of the
" evening, and the terrors which oppressed his
" mind in consequence of them. Rabby was
" prepared to receive him with all the gravity
" of a father-confessor. The landlord gave
" a full narration of the events, and of his
" own fears; which were wonderfully increas-
" ed by Robert's solemn commentaries. He
" represented to the terrified landlord, the
" danger he had to apprehend from attempt-
" ing to address his Maker in a state of in-
" toxication, and that he had reason to expect
" some serious affliction from the impropriety
" of his conduct. The landlord acknowledged
" his guilt, and promised amendment in fu-
" ture. Upon this acknowledgment and pro-

" mise, Robert absolved him, and recom-
" mended a night's rest as the most proper
" exercise for one in his condition.

" Notwithstanding, however, of this sup-
" posed preternatural warning, and the pro-
" mise of amendment, it was not long before
" the landlord relapsed into his usual habits;
" for, on the Saturday following, he came into
" his shop, at a late hour, almost incapable of
" attending to any thing. Robert was there,
" and after censuring him more severely than
" before, determined on playing him some
" other trick. An opportunity immediately
" offered, and it was embraced. A custo-
" mer sent for a sight of some goods, which
" the landlord packed up, and carried to the
" person's house. Robert, somewhat dis-
" guised, followed at a distance; waited con-
" cealed till the landlord came out; and, at a
" proper place, snatched away the goods, and
" left him to find the way home the best way
" he could. With the parcel, he reached
" the shop first, and having concealed it in a
" snug corner, was standing at his ease. The
" landlord, upon his return, wonderfully mag-
" nified the circumstances of the robbery, but
" seemed thankful that he was permitted to
" escape with life. Robert sympathised in his
" sorrows and joy, and all the family joined in

" the gratulations usual on such occasions.
" The next day being Sunday, a profound si-
" lence was observed by all parties; and by
" Monday morning Robert had made the ser-
" vants acquainted with what he had done,
" and his reasons for doing it. At the same
" time, he prepared a few lines, as from a
" most noted woman of bad fame, addressed
" to the landlord, intimating to him his irre-
" gular conduct in coming to her house in a
" disorderly manner, leaving his goods, seem-
" ingly incapable of taking care of himself;
" and adding, that from his years, and the
" character he ought to support, she was un-
" willing to expose him, and had returned his
" goods, with her friendly advice, *That he would*
" *be careful in future not to expose himself*. Ro-
" bert watched the landlord's approach, put
" the parcel of goods and note into his hands,
" and as the note was unsealed, the landlord
" naturally concluded, that all in the shop had
" perused it. He stood amazed; and return-
" ing the note to Fergusson, declared his in-
" nocence, earnestly requesting that the matter
" might be concealed. Robert gravely pe-
" rusing the note, seemed astonished at its con-
" tents, but would not listen to the landlord's
" plea of innocence. He told him, he had no
" intention of injuring him, by publishing the

" affair; and strongly recommended to him
" to profit by the friendly advice which the
" note contained; for he evidently saw, that
" in his intoxication, he neither knew where
" he had been, what he did, nor what was
" done to him. Many similar tricks and fro-
" lics Mr Fergusson engaged in, with a view
" to reclaim his landlord from the cup, but it
" is believed without success. In other re-
" spects the landlord was a good sort of man,
" and Mr Fergusson expressed a great regard
" for him. What was very singular too, the
" landlord was always giving Rabby (as he cal-
" led him) his best advice against *wildness;* sea-
" soning his advice with religious injunctions.

" Mr Fergusson seemed so violent against
" fanatics, and fanatical opinions and practices,
" that he seldom missed an opportunity of ex-
" posing those who were in any degree of this
" character. One Sunday, when passing by
" a Glassite meeting-house, he heard the con-
" gregation praising the Lord with all their
" might; and knowing somewhat of their e-
" vening practice of love feasts, &c. he placed
" himself on a stone adjoining the house, took
" a slip of paper and pencil from his pocket,
" and wrote some lines, in imitation of their
" canting jargon, which he carefully folded
" up, and threw in at an open window to those

" assembled. During Mr Fergusson's expe-
" ditions to the country (of which he was very
" fond), he was daily engaged in some harm-
" less frolic or humorous adventure. One day
" he somehow procured a sailor's habit, of the
" coarsest kind, in which he dressed himself;
" and, with a huge stick in his hand, he vi-
" sited a great number of his acquaintances.
" He was so effectually disguised, that few or
" none of them knew him ; and, by acquaint-
" ing many of them with some of their former
" transactions and conduct, he so much sur-
" prised them, that they imputed his know-
" ledge to divination. By this means he pro-
" cured from many of them such a fund of in-
" formation, as enabled him to give them a
" greater surprise, when he resumed the ge-
" nuine character of Robby Fergusson. For
" in the sailor's habit, he informed them of
" many frailties and failings, that they ima-
" gined impossible for one of his appearance
" to know ; and in the habit of Robby Fer-
" gusson, he divulged many things which they
" believed none but the ragged sailor was ac-
" quainted with."

These youthful frolics were not in themselves
worthy of much disapprobation : some of them,
on the contrary, give a favourable view of his
character, and indicate a happy union of cheer-

fulness and benevolence. They, however, were too often connected with circumstances of a nature inauspicious to the future welfare of youthful genius, and frequently the means of introducing him to scenes of the most pernicious influence. Whilst engaged in all the various gaieties of life to which he was exposed, he received from his brother Harry (who had changed a mercantile for a sea-faring life) a letter, which it cannot be improper to introduce into this memoir, as it illustrates at once the domestic attachments of Fergusson, and some particulars relative to a man connected to him by the ties of blood and affection. The letter is dated " Tartar, in Rapahannock Ri-" ver, Virginia, 8th of October, 1773.

" Since the beginning of last month, when
" I was favoured with yours of the 1st Febru-
" ary, 1773, I have been in most rivers in this
" province and Maryland. Our business was
" to look out after smugglers ; and had we
" been as active in that duty as others on the
" American station, I might have been en-
" abled to make my appearance in a brilliant
" manner ; but, alas ! only a sloop of eighty
" tons, from the West Indies, loaden with cof-
" fee and sugar, fell to our lot. I had sixteen
" dollars for my share, three of which I gave
" towards buying a tender, and every fore-

" mast-man paid one. The tender is now
" manned, armed, and cruizing Chesapeak bay,
" and I am convinced cannot fail of taking
" prizes, if the officers appointed for that duty
" are attentive.

" We had the most severe winter at Hali-
" fax ever experienced in that country. The
" harbour, though three miles across, was
" frozen over for three weeks. The ship's
" company walked aboard and ashore, nay,
" all our provisions were got aboard on the
" ice (which in many places was thirty-six feet
" in thickness), notwithstanding the strong
" north-west winds which blow most of the
" winter.

" When we arrived at Boston, we were or-
" dered to this country, which has been as hot
" this summer, as the former was cold in win-
" ter. Such a change of climate could not fail
" to create sickness in the ship's company;
" but, thank God, only three have died, one
" a natural death, and the other two drown-
" ed.

" I had a very severe fit of sickness at our first
" coming here; but being so much given to
" sweating, it proved an effectual cure, al-
" though I am very weak through that means.
" I never lived so badly as aboard here, in
" point of provisions, every species being the

" worst of their kinds, and neither butter nor
" flour to be had.

" I desire you will write by the packet on
" receipt ; for if you lay hold of any other op-
" portunity, your letter will be too late ; the
" ship being positively ordered home early
" next spring, to my great satisfaction, being
" quite tired of a life that my past follies drove
" me to, and to which I have served too long
" an apprenticeship. If every thing does not
" succeed to my satisfaction, on my arrival in
" England, I am fully bent to return and settle
" in this country ; having had the fairest offers
" imaginable, could my discharge have been
" procured. In Virginia and Maryland, in
" particular, I could do best by acting in a
" double capacity, by learning (teaching) the
" small sword, and the exercise of the small
" arms, there being no regular forces in either
" province, and the officers of the militia be-
" ing quite ignorant themselves of that part of
" their duty.

" I desire it as a favour, you would often
" examine your poetical pieces before you com-
" mit them to the press. This advice I hope
" you will the more readily take, as most
" young authors are apt to be more criticised
" than those who have had a little experience.
" Pope himself, was one of the most careful

46

" in this respect, and none as yet ever surpas-
" sed him. When I arrive in England, I shall
" give you the necessary directions how to send
" your works, and make no doubt of selling
" them to advantage, when the ship is paid
" off.

" I am sorry to hear of J. Wright's death:
" he was a worthy young lad, and one I had
" a true regard for.

" Thick Peter, I hope by this time is re-
" covered. I should be glad to hear of Ro-
" bertson and Addison's success: the latter,
" if in Edinburgh, I desire to be kindly re-
" membered to. I should also be happy to
" hear how Sandie Young, and John Coomans
" do, having often experienced their kindness,
" and been happy in their company.

" In our passage from Boston to Hampton,
" we had a very narrow escape with our lives,
" being surrounded with one of the largest
" water-spouts ever seen, which blackened
" the sky for some leagues; and, had we not
" barely weathered it, would have sunk the
" ship and every soul aboard.

" Remember me in the strongest manner
" to my mother, Peggy, Rarities, Father Park-
" er, &c. &c. If you want either to succeed,
" or gain esteem, be very careful of what com-
" pany you keep. This advice I hope you

" will take, as it comes from one who has lost
" himself merely through inattention in that
" respect. Believe me, it is impossible to
" write you as I would chuse, being environed
" with twenty thousand noisy plagues, not to
" mention execrations so horrid, that would
" make the greatest blackguard in Edinburgh's
" hair stand erect. I hope you'll make it your
" particular care, to study such branches of
" education as may prove most conducive to
" your future happiness, and appear at least
" once every Sunday in church (I mean the
" church of Scotland), for how can you spend
" your time better? I was, like many, fond
" of the church of England's forms, &c. but
" having been in many Romish churches since,
" find these forms are merely the * * * of la-
" ziness, and differ but very little from one
" another; this you can be convinced of, in
" perusing a Romish mass-book in English."

The following is also an extract of another
of his letters to his brother. The date is torn
away, but it appears to have been written from
Edinburgh.

" I read with attention, the burial-letter
" you versified, and your poetical letter to the
" cripple lauret. The former I approve of,
" but cannot recommend the latter in point of
" rhyme. You'll please notice, that the three

" first and fifth, and the second and fourth
" lines, in compositions of this kind (such as
" Habbie Simpson, &c.) chime with one ano-
" ther.

" At first when I came here, I imagined
" when one spoke of entering at a precise time,
" that he was serious; but now I see the con-
" trary, and that their promises are only to
" tantalize me; for ever since the year 1601,
" that the Court sat here, the Edinburghers
" have retained some of its fashions, and a-
" mong the rest, flattery to a high degree.

" I have only eight scholars, but expect
" more *. God grant they may not prove like
" one Campbell, who bilk'd me out of 2l. 2s.
" for instructions I gave him upon one foot.
" Although he has done me much evil, yet I
" shall not pray for him in the manner Paul,
" or some other apostle, did for Alexander
" the coppersmith."

It were an unpleasant and invidious task to
exhibit a full narrative of the dissipated scenes
in which Fergusson mingled. They were too
numerous to admit of being particularly de-
tailed, and too much alike, in their disgusting
features, to afford any gratification to the ad-

* He occasionally taught the use of the sword; and like-
wise published a treatise on that subject.

mirers of virtue and the friends of genius.
The censorious might, indeed, find ample
room for the indulgence of their spleen, and
the illiterate might triumph over the ruins of
dishonoured talents and learning ; but it is not
to such men that a consideration of Fergusson's
life can be useful. It is to such as stand in cir-
cumstances similar to those in which he was plac-
ed, that his errors speak from the grave with a
voice of thunder. No man in the outset of life can
survey the life of Robert Fergusson, without
shuddering at the practices which sullied his
existence ; or consider his latter end, without
sympathising in the horrors which conducted
him to the tomb.

The fashionable practices of society in this
part of the world, are perhaps the most fruit-
ful sources from whence our countrymen de-
rive their misery and their vice. Compared
with these causes of wretchedness, the natural
evils of existence, and the disadvantages of
social condition, are as dust in the balance.
Among others, the evils of conviviality are
immensely pernicious. In many cases, busi-
ness cannot be transacted, but over the glass :
the desirable intercourse of life, and the plea-
sures of hospitality, are thought by many to
be unattainable, except in the gratification of
intemperance. No man can avoid giving a

sanction in a greater or less degree to such habits, by his practice, however much he may disapprove of them in the abstract, unless, indeed, he is ready to incur the charge of singularity and affectation, or chuses to relinquish all the charms of social intercourse. Wisdom, however, is manifested in the discreet use of intoxicating beverage. Under its influence, the most delicate sensibility, the most rigid virtue, and inflexible firmness, cannot preserve a man from folly and from crime. In the gay season of youth, its power is doubly baleful. Fergusson is a striking example. His understanding was powerful ; his heart generous, even to weakness ; his feelings delicate, elevated, honourable ; his mind ardently glowed with the sublime emotions of religion : yet in the midst of the scenes of dissipation to which he was exposed, and in which he was admirably calculated to shine, his best qualities were humbled in the dust. Urged by the madening draught, prudence, reason, principle, all fell prostrate before the potent poison : he indulged in the gratification of animal passion, until his hapless career was closed in madness.

While his physical system was under the influence of medicine, for his recovery from the consequences of ebriety and folly, he was unfortunately enticed to accompany some gentlemen, who were interested in an election business, to one of the eastern counties of Scotland. On this expedition he was much exposed to the riotous enjoyments incident to such occasions ; and these, in conjunction with his disordered health, produced a feverishness and decrepitude of mind amounting nearly to insanity.

In stating these particulars, I only adhere to a resolution, which I formed at the time I thought of writing these pages, of suppressing no circumstance in the life of Robert Fergusson, that tended, in any degree, to illustrate his *real* character. It is my decided purpose, to tell the truth, and all the truth ; nor, in my apprehension, does the mention of the fact, now for the first time brought into view, cast a stain on the memory of Fergusson, which cannot be washed away. I do not affect to vindicate the mode of behaviour that he adopted ; which debilitated his body and impaired his intellectual powers : but I cannot be regarded as presumptuous, if I remind the precise herd of mankind, that a divine Advocate, in behalf of our infirmities, once checked the pharisaical sanctimony of noisy virtue. I do not ask forgetfulness of Fergusson's errors, by mentioning his youth, his fire, his inexperience. I do not speak of his merits and his misfortunes, as an apology for his follies. I cannot paint the delusions of hope and the rackings of disappointed ambition. But I call upon the censorious, and even the sincerely virtuous, to search their own bosoms, to examine their own feelings and temptations, and to review their own conduct. If in this process they can find no ground of self disapprobation, no trace of error, no instance of intemperance or misconduct, then shall I silently hear their exultations over the venial transgressions of Fergusson. But if they recollect any manifestations of human weakness in their own conduct, let them be satisfied with the obscurity of their vices, and not trample with puritanic pride upon that dust which Robert Burns has embalmed with his tears.

The state of Fergusson's mind, during this gloomy period of his existence, demands peculiar attention, ere we trace him to the close of his short career. It will be recollected, that Fergusson received a religious education. He had also been taught to assent to the peculiar doctrines of the Scotch church. There can be no doubt too, that he felt the " compunc- " tious visitings" of remorse, amid the scenes of riot in which he so often took a part: for the same ardour of mind which plunges a youth into the most extravagant licentiousness, is perhaps the best and most certain remedy for the evils which spring from it, if indeed these evils can be remedied. The constitution of mind and of body, which feels, with most vivid delight, the mad rapture of voluptuousness, will also suffer the gnawings of remorse with a keener anguish, a more efficacious regret, than can possibly take place in the tame, cautious, methodical debauchee. There is the best reason to believe, that superstitious horror, and wounded sensibility, co-operated in making Fergusson retire from the haunts of profligacy, and meditate, with a gloomy despondency, on the errors of his life. Whatever was the cause, the effect is certain : For a considerable time before his death, he laboured under the afflicting malady of religious, or rather superstitious horror. Various particulars have been mentioned, as the immediate fore-runners of this state of mind. I will not load my narrative with animadversions on the different accounts which have been given of the matter, but state what I am persuaded is most consistent with the truth, from a comparison of those accounts, and from the information which I have received through a gentleman well acquainted with Fergusson, who, indeed, must be regarded, as in this instance, the delineator of his own feelings and condition.

" In the month of December, 1773 (says
" the gentleman to whom I allude), I met
" with Mr Fergusson in Edinburgh, seemingly
" in good health, though I observed him to
" be more serious and thoughtful than former-
" ly : and in the month of March succeeding,
" I also met with him. He was then very
" poorly, and, in the course of a long walk,
" he freely communicated the state of his
" mind, and also the situation he had been in
" for some time." The substance of that con-
versation is partly given in the preceding pages,
being a detail of the circumstances connected
with the unfortunate complaint with which
Fergusson was afflicted, and his account of the
electioneering excesses in which he had par-
taken. He imputed the decayed state of his
body to these circumstances, and said, he was
afraid, that not this consequence alone had
arisen from them ; for he feared they had also
affected his head. He seemed, indeed, to be
quite aware that his mind was in disorder,
and he anticipated, with terror, the confine-
ment in a mad-house, which he foresaw would
be unavoidable.

He also introduced the Christian Religion,
and conversed with much earnestness on some

of its fundamental doctrines. Upon a particu-
lar occasion, which he specified, he said a Mr
Ferrier, at or near St Andrews, had alarmed
and rather displeased him, by maintaining
what are usually denominated the orthodox
tenets of our Scotch creeds: and Fergusson
appeared to differ, in a very considerable de-
gree, from the commonly received notions on
these subjects. He did not seem to be satis-
fied of the necessity of the fall of man, and
of a mediatorial sacrifice for human iniquity;
and he questioned, with considerable boldness,
the consistency of such doctrines, with the at-
tributes of divine wisdom and goodness. At
the same time, however, he confessed the im-
perfect nature of human intellect, and the un-
fathomable depth of all such enquiries. This
is the only gleam of infidelity which ever seems
to have diminished the fearful gloom of super-
stitious terror : no consoling rays of genuine
religion charmed his bosom ; no sounds of
peace gladdened his heart, and enabled him to
sustain, with fortitude and calmness, the sor-
rows which oppressed him. He anticipated
" the last peal of the thunder of heaven" as
the voice of Eternal Vengeance speaking in
wrath, and consigning him to irremediable
perdition. Fergusson's religion, at this time,
was the religion of a man in despair. His in-

fidelity was a burst of fancy, and the melancholy effort of a freezing energy of reason, which enabled him to hope for peace in the gulph of annihilation, when that of eternal torture seemed yawning to receive him.

It has been said by some of his biographers, that the religious despondency which afflicted Fergusson, arose from a conversation with the late Reverend Mr John Brown of Haddington—a man eminent for his acquaintance with sacred literature, and for the laborious and zealous application of his knowledge, in the discharge of his pastoral functions. The whole amount of this story is as follows:

Mr Brown, when taking a walk in Haddington church-yard, met with a disconsolate gentleman, whom he did not know, walking in the same place. Having met, they accosted one another; and Mr Brown took occasion, from the nature of the place, to make a few remarks on the mortality of man—observing, that in a short time they would be soon laid in the dust, and that, therefore, it was wise to prepare for eternity. The conversation did not last above three or four minutes, and was not considered by Mr Brown, at least, as of much importance. This disconsolate gentleman, it seems, was Fergusson; and the above rencounter happened, it is believed, in 1772, although the precise period does not seem to be perfectly known. A very triffling circumstance will, in particular situations and states of the mind, produce extraordinary consequences. There is, however, little evidence, that Fergusson was so suddenly awakened to a sense of mortality, and so deeply impressed with anxiety about a future existence, by this occurrence, as has been supposed. He must have heard the same truths resounded in his ears a thousand times before; and we may safely conclude, that the impression which it made on his mind was very trifling, since even his daily associates never discovered any alteration in the tone of his feelings. The truth upon this point seems to be, that a variety of circumstances, at the same period, contributed to excite his superstitious melancholy. His injudicious conduct enfeebled his body; his consciousness of error must have been as vivid as his ardour in the pursuit of licentious pleasure was extreme; and these causes, in combination with the power of early associations, and the arousing circumstances which are known to have existed, co-operated for the production of that state of mind which we are now contemplating.

The crisis of Fergusson's fate now approached. A short interval of tranquillity occurred,

and enabled him once more to mingle in the
social riot. On one occasion, as he was going
home, he fell from a stair-case, and received
a violent contusion on the head. When
carried to his mother's house, he could
give no account of the manner in which
the accident had befallen him, and seemed
totally insensible of his deplorable condi-
tion. He soon arrived at a state of the most
frantic madness. His situation was humiliat-
ing to the pride of human genius. He lay
stretched on a humble bed, surrounded with
the appaling insignia of a lunatic asylum. The
smile of complacency, and generosity, and
worth, which was wont to animate his coun-
tenance, had given place to the haggard wild-
ness of aspect which distinguishes the maniac.
Fergusson, in the humbled state to which he
was now reduced, frequently sang with a pa-
thos and tenderness of expression which he
never surpassed in the happiest moments of
his convivial brilliancy : in particular, he
chaunted " The Birks of Invermay" with such
exquisite melody, that those who heard his
notes can never forget the sound.

The pecuniary circumstances of Mrs Fergus-
son were so limited, and the means or inclina-
tion of her son's reputed friends so circumscrib-
ed, that it was found necessary to remove him

to the public asylum, for the reception of per-
sons in his situation. This was an unfortunate
necessity for Fergusson. By a judicious atten-
tion to his disordered mind, it might have
been healed, and restored to the world : for
his madness was not constitutional insanity,
but the result of high sensibility, wounded and
exasperated by disease and misfortune.

A deception, cruel and barbarous in the ex-
treme, and unjustifiable upon any ground of
expedience or necessity, was practised for his
removal to the asylum. A few of his most
intimate associates pretended that they wished
him to go on a visit to an acquaintance ; and,
having got him placed in a sedan chair, they
conducted him to the asylum. He soon dis-
covered the place to which he was consigned,
and uttered a scream of horror and despair,
which was re-echoed by the commingled yell-
ings of this mansion of wretchedness.

Heard ye that piercing maniac shriek,
　　That awful, wild, responsive yell,
Dread as Despair's first notes, that shook
　　The dreary dark concave of hell ?

Strike ! strike the harp, the deepest tone
　　That ever plaintive pity knew :
Fallen genius ! thine the frantic groan—
　　Thus hail'd thy steps the phrenzied crew.

But softer notes—hark ! hark again,
   The melting sounds of settled woe :
Sweet Invermay, thy plaintive strains,
   In wildly thrilling accents flow.

The voice that charm'd the festive board,
   On which the ear enraptur'd hung—
'Twas his—'twas Fergusson's I heard,
   One of the sweetest sons of song.

Where is that wit, in other days,
   That flash'd around the social board,
That gilded with its meteor blaze,
   The scenes thy better sense abhorr'd ?

Where are the smiles thou wont to wear ?
   A settled gloom their place supplies :
The vacant gaze, the frantic stare—
   Now the sole language of those eyes.

Ah ! in that sad and gloomy hour,
   When reason left her wonted seat,
Why could not friendship's willing power
   Supply a more benign retreat ;

Where cheering as the rays of Heaven,
   A mother's or a sister's voice,
Horror's black clouds might far have driven,
   And charm'd thee back to social joys ?

Friendship ! sweet tie among the good,
   Let not the sons of riot claim :
Chaste love ! they blast it in the bud,
   And friendship blooms an empty name.

They left thee, Fergusson, to want,—disease ;
No friendly hand e'en mark'd thy grave,
Till kindred genius traced the sacred place,
What Burns now needs to thee he gave *.

The circumstances attending Fergusson's confinement, are so briefly and so interestingly stated by Mr Irving and Mr Sommers, that I cannot present them to the reader more completely, than by transcribing a few passages of their respective memoirs.

" During the first night of his confine-
" ment (says Mr Sommers), he slept none ;
" and when the keeper visited him in the
" morning, he found him walking along the
" stone floor of his cell, with his arms fold-
" ed, and in sullen sadness, uttering not a
" word. After some minutes silence, he
" clapped his right hand on his forehead, and
" complained much of pain. He asked the
" keeper, who brought him there ? He answer-
" ed, Friends.—Yes, friends, indeed, replied
" Robert, they think I am too wicked to live,
" but you will soon see me a *shining and a burn-*
" *ing light.* You have been so already, ob-

* These lines were written on a perusal of the present sketch, and sent with the manuscript to the writer, by a much valued friend, who has given his consent to the publication of them.

" served the keeper *. You mistake me, said
" the Poet: I mean you shall see and hear of
" me as a bright minister of the gospel!"

Mr Irving tells us, that " when he was af-
" terwards visited by his mother and elder sis-
" ter, his phrensy had almost entirely subsided.
" He had at first imagined himself a king or
" some other great personage; and adorned
" his head with a crown of straw, which he
" plaited very neatly with his own hands. The
" delusion, however, was now vanished: upon
" their entering, they found him lying in his
" cell, to appearance calm and collected. He
" told them he was sensible of their kindness,
" and hoped he should soon be in a condition
" to receive their visits. He also recalled to
" their memory the presentiment which he
" had so often expressed, of his being at length
" overwhelmed by this most dreadful of all
" calamities; but endeavoured to comfort
" them with assurances of his being humanely
" treated in the asylum. He entreated his
" sister to bring her work, and frequently sit
" by him, in order to dispel the gloom that
" overcast his mind. To all this they could
" only answer with their sighs and tears.—
" When the keeper entered, and informed
" them that it was time to depart, he with

* Alluding to his Poems.

" great earnestness conjured them to remain
" with him a little longer : but with this re-
" quest it was not in their power to comply.
" From his behaviour during this interview,
" his mother was led to entertain hopes of his
" speedy recovery."

" Day after day, I inquired for him (says
" Mr Sommers) of his mother and younger
" sister, but never had resolution to pay him
" a personal visit. After, however, nearly two
" months had elapsed, I was surprised at hear-
" ing of his being still in his captive state, and
" therefore was determined to give him a call,
" but found that it was necessary to obtain,
" for that purpose, an order in writing from
" the sitting magistrate. In my way to the
" Council Chamber, to procure the order, I met
" with Dr John Aitken, late physician here ;
" I told him where I was going, and for what
" purpose. He expressed a wish to accom-
" pany me, as he knew the Poet well. Both
" our names were inserted in the Magistrate's
" mandate of admission, with a promise, on
" the part of the Doctor, to report to the
" Magistrate the state of the Poet. We got
" immediate access to the cell, and found Ro-
" bert lying with his clothes on, stretched up-
" on a bed of loose uncovered straw. The
" moment he heard my voice, he instantly a-

" rose, got me in his arms, and wept. The
" Doctor felt his pulse, and declared it to be
" favourable. I asked the keeper (whom I
" formerly knew as a gardener) to allow him
" to accompany us into an adjoining back
" court, by way of taking the air. He con-
" sented. Robert took hold of me by the
" arm, placing me on his right, and the Doc-
" tor on his left, and in this form we walked
" backward and forward along the court, con-
" versing for nearly an hour; in the course of
" which, many questions were asked at him
" both by the Doctor and myself, to which
" he returned most satisfactory answers; but
" seemed very anxious to obtain his liberty.

" Having passed about two hours with him
" on this visit, we found it necessary to take
" our leave, the Doctor assuring him, that he
" would soon be restored to his friends, and
" that I would visit him again in a day or two.
" He calmly, and without a murmur, walked
" with us to the cell, and upon parting, re-
" minded the Doctor of his promise, to get him
" soon at liberty, and of mine, to see him next
" day. Neither of us, however, had an oppor-
" tunity of accomplishing our promise; for in
" a few days thereafter, I received an intima-
" tion from the keeper, that Robert Fergusson
" had breathed his last," &c.

This event took place after he had continued about two months in confinement. Fergusson expired in the solitude of his cell, amid the terrors of the night, " without a hand " to help, or an eye to pity." His dying couch was a mat of straw. The last sounds which pealed upon his ear, were the howlings of insanity. No tongue whispered peace ; and even a consoling tear of sympathy mingled not with those of contrition and of hope, which, in charity, I trust, illumined his closing eye.

Robert Fergusson died on the 16th of October 1774, very soon after he had completed his twenty-fourth year ; and a few days afterwards, his body was buried in the Canongate church-yard. His grave remained almost undistinguished from those of the multitude by which it was surrounded, until Robert Burns appeared in Edinburgh (1787) to eclipse his fame, and to follow his career. When he came to Fergusson's grave, he uncovered his head, and kneeling down in a transport of enthusiasm, clasped the venerated clay to his ardent bosom. He obtained leave from the Magistrates of Canongate to erect a monument on the spot. It is now to be seen, a plain, yet splendid, mark of the generosity of Burns's character.

" No sculptur'd marble here, nor pompous lay,
" No storied urn nor animated bust,
" This simple stone directs pale Scotia's way,
" To pour her sorrows o'er her Poet's dust *."

If Fergusson had lived only a few days long-
er than he did, the aspect of his life would
most probably have been changed by the ope-
ration of circumstances not connected with
barren friendships. His mother had been en-
abled, by the receipt of a remittance from her
son Henry, to arrange her household in such
a manner as to prepare for Robert a comfort-
able release from his dungeon. If her pur-
pose had been effected, there can be little
doubt that his future sanity was a probable cir-
cumstance, and that his after life would have
been as much distinguished for sobriety and
prudence, as his youth had been for jollity and
thoughtlessness. He had been able to ascer-
tain the emptiness of licentious pleasure, and
to estimate the friendship of those men for
whose society he had sacrificed his health and
every thing which could have rendered his life

* This is the epitaph which Burns engraved on his tomb.
On the reverse side of the stone, is the following inscription:

" By special grant of the Managers
" To ROBERT BURNS, who erected this Stone,
" This burial place is ever to remain sacred to the memory of
" ROBERT FERGUSSON."

useful and honourable. Although caressed by multitudes in the day of his glory, he was neglected when " shorn of his beams," and permitted to expire in the common receptacle for the most friendless wretches of society. Many of his associates, no doubt, were disqualified, by their situations in life, from assisting him materially in any of the calamitous events which befel him ; but still Fergusson will stand a striking example of what every man may expect in the hour of misfortune—the indifference and the censure of many who participated in his follies, but who never conferred any essential favour on him. From this reflection, one name deserves to be exempted. A Mr Burnet had felt such an attachment to the genius and heart of Fergusson, that upon his settlement in India, he was desirous of promoting the interests of his friend. He accordingly sent an invitation to him to come over to India, and, at the same time, remitted a draft for L. 100, to defray the expences of the outward voyage. Fergusson was dead ere these testimonies of friendship arrived. If he had lived no longer than to know of this solitary instance of disinterested benevolence, he would have left the world with the satisfaction arising from the certainty of human worth ; a certainty which he could scarcely be supposed to feel,

with consolatory ardour, when he retraced the
progress of his life, and trembled amid the gloom
and the miseries of a common mad-house.

> Oft has the Muse bedew'd with tears, the urn
> Of Genius and Misfortune—oft her song
> In deepest numbers breath'd the hapless tale ;
> For many a heart which beat with heavenly thought,
> And many a hand, with energy divine
> That struck the lyre, hath sunk into the tomb.—
> But never since the rapid flood of time
> Began to roll, the record of man's ills,—
> Sure, never since that hour when first he dared
> To wish himself a God, and spurned the earth,
> Has Genius lift its eagle eye to heaven
> Thro' darker clouds of sorrow and despair
> Than o'er my country's youthful Bard were hung !
>   Be mine the willing task, a sorrowing verse
> To weave around his tomb, whose worth and woes
> Remain almost unsung.   Oh FERGUSSON,
> For thee and for thy sufferings I mourn !
> The journey of thy life was short, and round
> Thy narrow path the world was wilderness :
> No smiling joys thy future prospect cheer'd,
> And hollow Friendship's hand beguil'd thy steps
> To ruin.   Even the passing moment passed
> A hectic dream of joyous suffering :
> For tho' beneath thy feet some flow'rets bloom'd,
> Diffusing pleasure's honied fragrance, still
> Each blossom fair conceal'd a thorn :
> What tho' around thee Flattery's incense rose,
> When every breathing wafted pestilence ?
> What tho' thy Genius soar'd aloft at times
> With flight angelic ? madness brought thee low.

Ah! who can trace the deep, deep hidden source
Of the etherial poison of the soul,
Subtle, resistless, bursting as from heaven
To blast the fairest offspring of its will?
The bosom of the deep, convuls'd, may heave
In vast commotion, and the rain descend
In dashing cataracts: the whirlwind's voice
May join its angry roar: the sun obscur'd
In night-like day, may sadden Nature's brow:
The thunder sheet may gleam o'erhead, and clothe
The firmament in universal flame;
And heaven, and earth, and seas, and skies appear
In one wild uproar blending—yet can Man
Survey, contemplate, and describe the scene.
But the confusion of the soul—the mind
Diseased—the spirit broken—and the gloom
Of superstition's horror, who can paint,
With tints celestial and a hand of fire,
Or tell, with inspiration's seraph tongue,
Thy pangs, oh FERGUSSON! thy speechless woe?

I think thou art a Friend.   What tho' the grave
Forbids thy dust to look on mine, and mark
The sympathies which bind man's soul to man
In earthly union? Still my heart can claim
A kindred to the throbbing pulse of thine.—
I love thee in that grave.   The sepulchre
Yields up its empire o'er thy mind.
Altho' its morning's early ray was dimm'd
By error's shades, and tho' ere long 'twas quench'd
In death's o'ershadowing gloom, it leaves behind
A stream of brightness.—If the trembling eye
Can view the sun descending in the blaze
Of majesty expiring, it beholds
A mimic image of his form, when sunk
Beneath th' horizon's verge his glories fly
To cherish other regions of the world.—

The Poet thus, when ravish'd from our sphere,
Still shines in other realms,—the realms of day ;
And, like the sun, some image still remains
Sav'd from the yawning darkness of his tomb.

After perusing the narrative which has now
been given, the mind pauses with involuntary
solemnity, to contemplate the images which it
exhibits. In Robert Fergusson and his fate,
there is a mixture of what delights, with what
distresses. His character, whether as a man
or a poet, displays many of the most inte-
resting qualities of which human nature can
boast ; but they were blended with the im-
perfections which have too often clouded the
brightest effulgence of genius. Yet his virtues,
though numerous, have been lost amid the
darkness of demerits, created by the power of
imagination.

Mr Irving has unwarily, to say the least of
it, blotted his page with an error of the gross-
est kind. He tells us, in the earlier editions
of his memoir, that Fergusson's " dissipated
" manner of life, had in a great measure era-
" dicated all sense of delicacy or propriety ;"
and, in the edition of 1804 *, we have the
same assertion somewhat varied, but aggra-
vated by the intolerable solemnity of the state-

* Pages 421 and 422.

ment. " His latter years (says Mr Irving)
" were wasted in *perpetual dissipation.* The con-
" dition to which he had reduced himself, pre-
" pared him for grasping at every object which
" promised a temporary alleviation of his cares ;
" and as his funds were often in an exhausted
" state, *he at length had recourse to mean expedi-*
" *ents.*" Language such as this, can neither
be misunderstood nor explained away. It
pourtrays a bold and strongly coloured picture
of human depravity, such as seems to require
very decisive evidence of its truth. But Mr
Irving has given no testimony—he has not
mentioned a single name to accompany his own
in a statement that is calculated to stamp in-
famy on the memory of an unfortunate man
of genius, nor has he even specified the facts
from whence his general conclusion seems to
be drawn. I rejoice in being able to con-
trovert Mr Irving's affirmation. I am au-
thorised, by the concurring testimony of dif-
ferent individuals who knew Fergusson, to
contradict the assertions of Mr Irving, who
knew him not. Their evidence, indeed, is of
a negative kind, but I am well entitled to
found upon it as unchallengeable, until Mr
Irving has substituted positive proof in the
stead of palpable hypothesis. That his alle-
gation is a mere theoretical reverie, I am much

inclined to believe; for I cannot suppose him capable of a deliberate calumny. Mr Irving seems to imagine, that Fergusson was wicked and mean, because he was dissipated and poor. This is like the logic of a fanatical methodist, or of a recluse; but it is not the language of a man who has looked into the world, and taken an accurate and a liberal view of his fellow men. Poverty was Robert Fergusson's inheritance: his dissipation, which exceeded not the common errors of youth, arose from circumstances in which it never can be the lot of many to be placed; for it arose from the attractive charms of his genius. A generous mind will make allowance for the fascinations of flattery and the yielding simplicity of youth, amid the blandishments of the world : it will not regard his errors as proofs of his genius; neither will it indulge in contumelious invective; but it will sigh over the tomb of Fergusson, and indulge in those emotions with which we survey magnificence in disorder and in ruin.

In the domestic relations of life, Fergusson's conduct was exemplary, as far as his convivial irregularity admitted. Indeed, it would have been unexceptionable, had not these distracted the benevolent tendencies of his disposition, and led him to waste on the idle and dissipated, those affections which would have added a bright ray of sunshine to his existence, had their influence been confined within the range of domestic duties and enjoyment.

The personal appearance of Fergusson is described as interesting and genteel, although not peculiarly handsome. The only picture ever made of him, was by the celebrated Runciman, in the character of the Prodigal Son. The painting was excellent, and the countenance bore a striking resemblance to that of Fergusson : it was exhibited at the Royal Institution in London, and afterwards sold at a considerable price ; but it is not known by whom it was purchased, nor if it be still in existence. Like most men of sense, Fergusson despised the trappings of dress ; and like many men of genius, he laughed at those who made the form of their habiliments an object of deep importance.

It has been a common practice among the biographers of literary men, and particularly of poets, to interweave the history of their writings with that of their lives, and to connect critical disquisition with the details of fact. It is impossible, however, to exhibit any chronological account of the composition or publication of Fergusson's poems : the greater number of them were originally published in Ruddiman's Weekly Magazine, and first collected by himself, into a small volume, in 1773. After his death, a fuller edition, comprising several posthumous pieces, was published; and since that time they have passed through a nameless variety of editions. The public voice has already given its decision in favour of the poetic talent of Fergusson. I cannot recommend the beauties of his poems more powerfully than by presenting them for perusal: their blemishes are now sacred from criticism; for it cannot remove them. I at least feel no disposition to commence critic, but shall merely exercise the privilege of a biographer, in briefly delineating what I conceive to be the peculiar qualities of his genius and compositions.

Every circumstance of Fergusson's life indicates that ardent and susceptible temperament of constitution, which is perhaps the only ingredient of the poetic mind that is the gift of nature. By the education which he received, his natural sensibility seems to have been modified into the morbid refinement which is necessary for the creation of a poet—that delicacy of feeling which makes every surrounding object affect the mind in the way that leads to the various excellencies of poetry. Butler must have been peculiarly alive to the impressions of the grotesque and the ludicrous, before he could have written Hudibras: Pope or Churchill could never have poured out the torrent of invective, or pointed the cutting irony, unless a cynical susceptibility of disgust had characterised their minds; and Milton, assuredly, could never have ascended to the sublimities of Paradise Lost, unless his heart had often beat high with the conceptions of the great, the awful, and the magnificent. Fergusson, too, possessed a mental constitution, which made him strongly feel the influence of the circumstances in which he was placed; for the evidences of his genius bear the stamp of a mind which could distinguish and feel when the vulgar gazed with stupid insensibility. He was indeed a true poet: he united exquisite powers of observation with goodness of heart, and a fancy boundless in its range. He surveyed the face of nature, and she stamped her image on his soul. He looked around him on mankind, and his eye penetrated the recesses of the human heart. As a scholar, he drank from the stream of inspiration, in the hallowed source of ancient poesy, and, in this respect, his advantage over Burns was decisive: yet, although his muse often sports with equal sprightliness and vivacity, and sometimes soars with an elevated sweep, she seldom, like the mighty genius of Burns, darts impetuous and sublime. Fergusson's poems, however, it must be remembered, are now before the world with those imperfections which arise from youth and immaturity of judgment—from the temporary purposes which they were intended to serve, and the irregularity of the life during which they were written. They are to be regarded rather as the marks of genius, than as the models of excellence which it is capable of producing. They are the " glorious dawnings" of a mind which, ere it enlightened the world with its meridian splendour, was obscured, clouded, extinguished—obscured by the accidental humbleness of its social sphere, clouded by the misfortunes which hung around its mortal condition, and extinguished, by the darkness of the tomb, in its flight to eternity.

POEMS.

LYRICAL PIECES.

ODE TO HOPE.

Hope ! lively cheerer of the mind,
In lieu of real bless design'd,
Come from thy ever verdant bow'r
To chase the dull and lingering hour :
O ! bring, attending on thy reign,
All thy ideal fairy train,
To animate the lifeless clay,
And bear my sorrows hence away.

Hence, gloomy-featur'd black Despair,
 With all thy frantic furies, fly,
Nor rend my breast with gnawing care,
 For Hope in lively garb is nigh.

Let pining Discontentment mourn ,
  Let dull-ey'd Melancholy grieve ;
Since pleasing Hope must reign by turn,
  And every bitter thought relieve.

  O smiling Hope ! in adverse hour,
  I feel thy influencing pow'r.
  Tho' frowning Fortune fix my lot
  In some defenceless lonely cot,
  Where Poverty, with empty hands,
  In pallid meagre aspect stands ;
  Thou canst enrobe me 'midst the great,
  With all the crimson pomp of state,
  Where Luxury invites his guests
  To pall them with his lavish feasts.
  What cave so dark, what gloom so drear,
  So black with horror, dead with fear,
  But thou canst dart thy streaming ray,
  And change close night to open day ?

Health is attendant in thy radiant train ;
  Round her the whispering zephyrs gently
      play ;
Behold her gladly tripping o'er the plain,
  Bedeck'd with rural sweets and garlands gay !

  When vital spirits are deprest,
  And heavy languor clogs the breast,

With more than Esculapian power
Endu'd, bless'd Hope! 'tis thine to cure;
For oft thy friendly aid avails,
When all the strength of physic fails.

Nay, ev'n tho' death should aim his dart,
  I know he lifts his arm in vain,
Since thou this lesson canst impart,
  Mankind but die to live again.

Depriv'd of thee must banners fall:
  But where a living Hope is found,
The legions shout at danger's call,
  And victors are triumphant crown'd.

Come then, bright Hope! in smiles array'd,
  Revive us by thy quickening breath;
Then shall we never be afraid
  To walk thro' danger and thro' death.

THE RIVERS OF SCOTLAND,

AN ODE.

Set to Music by Mr Collett.

O'ER Scotia's parched land the Naiads flew,
   From towering hills explor'd her shelter'd
      vales,
Caus'd *Forth* in wild meanders please the view,
   And lift her waters to the zephyrs gales ;
Where the glad swain surveys his fertile fields,
And reaps the plenty which his harvest yields.

   Here did these lovely nymphs, unseen,
     Oft wander by the river's side,
   And oft unbind their tresses green,
     To bathe them in the fluid tide ;
Then to the shady grottos would retire,
And sweetly echo to the warbling choir ;

Or to the rushing waters tune their shells,
  To call up Echo from the woods,
  Or from the rocks or crystal floods,
Or from surrounding banks, or hills, or dales.

CHORUS.

Or to the rushing waters tune their shells,
  To call up Echo from the woods,
  Or from the rocks or crystal floods,
Or from surrounding banks, or hills, or dales.

When the cool fountains first their springs forsook,
  Murmuring smoothly to the azure main,
Exulting Neptune then his trident shook,
  And wav'd his waters gently to the plain.
The friendly Tritons on his chariot borne,
With cheeks dilated, blew the hollow-sounding
      horn.

Now Lothian and Fifan shores,
  Resounding to the Mermaid's song,
Gladly emit their limpid stores,
  And bid them smoothly sail along
To Neptune's empire, and with him to roll
Round the revolving sphere from pole to pole,

To guard Britannia from her envious foes;
  To view her angry vengeance hurl'd
  In awful thunder round the world,
And trembling nations bending to her blows.

CHORUS.

To guard Britannia from her envious foes;
  To view her angry vengeance hurl'd
  In awful thunder round the world,
And trembling nations bending to her blows.

High towering on the zephyr's breezy wing,
  Swift fly the Naiads from Fortha's shores,
And to the southern airy mountains bring
    Their sweet enchantment and their magic
      powers.

    Each nymph her favourite willow takes;
      The earth with fev'rous tremor shakes;
    The stagnant lakes obey their call;
      Streams o'er the grassy pastures fall.
Tweed spreads her waters to the lucid ray;
Upon the dimpled surf the sun-beams play.

On her green banks the tuneful shepherd lies
  Charmed with the music of his reed,
  Amidst the wavings of the Tweed:
From sky-reflecting streams the river-nymphs
      arise.

CHORUS.

On her green banks the tuneful shepherd lies
  Charm'd with the music of his reed,

Amidst the wavings of the Tweed :
From sky-reflecting streams the river-nymphs
    arise.

The listening Muses heard the shepherd's play :
  Fame with her brazen trump proclaim'd his
    name,
And to attend the easy graceful lay,
  Pan from Arcadia to Tweeda came.
Fond of the change, along the banks he stray'd,
And sung unmindful of the Arcadian shade.

AIR—*Tweedside.*

1

Attend every fanciful swain,
  Whose notes softly flow from the reed ;
With harmony guide the sweet strain,
  To sing of the beauties of Tweed.

2

Where the music of woods and of streams
  In soothing sweet melody join,
To enliven your pastoral themes,
  And make human numbers divine.

CHORUS.

Ye warblers from the vocal grove,
The tender woodland strain approve,

While Tweed in smoother cadence glides
O'er flowery vales in gentle tides ;
And as she rolls her silver waves along,
Murmurs and sighs to quit the rural song.
Scotia's great genius in russet clad,
From the cool sedgy bank exalts her head ;
In joyful rapture she the change espies ;
Sees living streams descend, and groves arise.

AIR—*Gilderoy.*

1

As sable clouds at early day
 Oft dim the shining skies ;
So gloomy thoughts create dismay,
 And lustre leaves her eyes.

2

" Ye powers ! are Scotia's ample fields
 " With so much beauty grac'd,
" To have those sweets your bounty yields
 " By foreign foes defac'd ?

3

" O Jove ! at whose supreme command
 " The limpid fountains play,
" O'er Caledonia's northern land
 " Let restless waters stray.

4

" Since from the void creation rose,
  " Thou'st made a sacred vow,
" That Caledon to foreign foes
  " Should ne'er be known to bow."

The mighty thunderer on his sapphire throne,
In mercy's robes attir'd, heard the sweet voice
Of female woe,—soft as the moving song
Of Philomela 'midst the evening shades ;
And thus returned an answer to her prayers :

  " Where birks at Nature's call arise ;
  " Where fragrance hails the vaulted skies ;
  " Where my own oak its umbrage spreads,
  " Delightful 'midst the woody shades ;
  " Where ivy-mouldering rocks entwines ;
  " Where breezes bend the lofty pines :
  " There shall the laughing Naiads stray,
  " 'Midst the sweet banks of winding Tay."

From the dark womb of earth Tay's waters
          spring,
  Ordain'd by Jove's unalterable voice ;
The sounding lyre celestial muses string ;
  The choiring songsters in the groves rejoice.

  Each fount its crystal fluids pours,
    Which from surrounding mountains flow ;

The river bathes its verdant shores ;
Cool o'er the surf the breezes blow.

Let England's sons extol their gardens fair ;
  Scotland may freely boast her generous
    streams ;
Their soil more fertile, and their milder air ;
  Her fishes sporting in the solar beams.
Thames, Humber, Severn, all must yield the
    bay
To the pure streams of Forth, of Tweed, and
    Tay.

CHORUS.

Thames, Humber, Severn, all must yield the
    bay
To the pure streams of Forth, of Tweed, and
    Tay.

O Scotia ! when such beauty claims
A mansion near thy flowing streams,
Ne'er shall stern Mars, in iron car,
Drive his proud coursers to the war ;
But fairy forms shall strew around
Their olives on the peaceful ground ;
And turtles join the warbling throng,
To usher in the morning song ;
Or shout in chorus all the live-long day,
From the green banks of Forth, of Tweed,
    and Tay.

When gentle Phœbe's friendly light
In silver radiance clothes the night,
Still Music's ever-varying strains
Shall tell the lovers, Cynthia reigns;
And woo them to her midnight bowers,
Among the fragrant dew-clad flowers,
Where every rock, and hill, and dale,
With echoes greet the nightingale,
Whose pleasing, soft, pathetic tongue,
To kind condolence turns the song;
And often wins the love-sick swain to stray,
To hear the tender variegated lay,
Thro' the dark woods of Forth, of Tweed, and
      Tay.

Hail, native streams, and native groves!
Oozy caverns, green alcoves!
Retreats for Cytherea's reign,
With all the graces in her train:
Hail, Fancy! thou whose ray so bright
Dispels the glimmering taper's light!
Come in aerial vesture blue,
Ever pleasing, ever new;
In these recesses deign to dwell
With me in yonder moss-clad cell:
Then shall my reed successful tune the lay,
In numbers wildly warbling as they stray
Thro' the glad banks of Forth, of Tweed, and
      Tay.

ODE TO PITY.

To what sequestered gloomy shade
Hath ever-gentle Pity strayed ?
What brook is watered from her eyes ?
What gales convey her tender sighs ?
Unworthy of her grateful lay,
She hath despised the great, the gay ;
Nay, all the feelings she imparts
Are far estranged from human hearts.

Ah, Pity ! whither wouldest thou fly
From human heart, from human eye ?
Are desert woods, and twilight groves,
The scenes the sobbing pilgrim loves ?
If there thou dwell'st, O Pity ! say,
In what lone path you pensive stray ?
I'll know thee by the lily's hue,
Besprinkled with the morning's dew :
For thou wilt never blush to wear
The pallid look and falling tear.

In broken cadence from thy tongue
Oft have we heard the mournful song ;
Oft have we view'd the loaded bier
Bedewed with Pity's softest tear.

Her sighs and tears were ne'er denied,
When innocence and virtue died.
But in this black and iron age,
Where Vice and all his demons rage,
Tho' bells in solemn peals are rung,
Tho' dirge in mournful verse is sung,
Soon will the vain parade be o'er,
Their name, their memory, no more,
Who love and innocence despised,
And every virtue sacrificed.
Here Pity, as a statue, dumb,
Will pay no tribute to the tomb ;
Or wake the memory of those
Who never felt for others woes.

   Thou mistress of the feeling heart !
Thy powers of sympathy impart.
If mortals would but fondly prize
Thy falling tears, thy passing sighs ;
Then should wan Poverty no more
Walk feebly from the rich man's door ;
Humility should banish Pride,
And Vice be drove from Virtue's side :
Then Happiness at length should reign ;
The golden age begin again.

ODE TO HORROR.

O THOU, who, with incessant gloom,
Courtest the recess of midnight tomb!
Admit me of thy mournful throng,
The scattered woods and wilds among.
If e'er thy discontented ear
The voice of sympathy can cheer,
My melancholy bosom's sigh
Shall to your mournful plaint reply ;
There to the fear-foreboding owl
The angry furies hiss and howl ;
Or near the mountain's pendant brow,
Where rush-clad streams in cadent murmurs
  flow.

EPODE.

Who's he, that, with imploring eye,
Salutes the rosy dawning sky ?
The cock proclaims the morn in vain,
His sprite to drive to its domain ;
For morning light can but return,
To bid the wretched wail and mourn.

Not the bright dawning's purple eye
Can cause the frightful vapours fly;
Nor sultry Sol's meridian throne
Can bid surrounding fears begone.
The gloom of night will still preside,
While angry conscience stares on either side.

STROPHE.

To ease his sore distempered head,
Sometimes upon the rocky bed
Reclined he lies, to list the sound
Of whispering reed in vale profound.
Happy, if Morpheus visits there,
A while to lull his woe and care;
Send sweeter fancies to his aid,
And teach him to be undismay'd;
Yet wretched still; for when no more
The gods their opiate balsam pour,
Behold! he starts, and views again
The Lybian monster prance along the plain.
 Now from the oozing caves he flies,
And to the city's tumults hies,
Thinking to frolic life away,
Be ever cheerful, ever gay:
But, tho' enwrapped in noise and smoke,
They ne'er can heal his peace, when broke.
His fears arise, he sighs again
For solitude on rural plain;

Even there his wishes all convene
To bear him to his noise again.
Thus tortur'd, rack'd, and sore opprest,
He constant hunts, but never finds his rest.

ANTISTROPHE.

O Exercise! thou healing power,
The toiling rustic's chiefest dower;
Be thou with heav'n-born virtue joined,
To quell the tumults of the mind;
Then, man as much of joy can share
From ruffian Winter, bleakly bare,
As from the pure ethereal blaze
That wantons in the Summer rays.
The humble cottage then can bring
Content, the comfort of a king;
And gloomy mortals wish no more
For wealth and idleness to make them poor.

ODE TO DISAPPOINTMENT.

Thou joyless fiend! life's constant foe;
Malignant source of care and woe,
        Pleasure's abhorred controul;

Her gayest haunts for ever nigh;
Stern mistress of the secret sigh,
    That swells the murmuring soul.

Why hauntest thou me thro' deserts drear?
With grief-swoln sounds why woundest my ear,
    Denied to Pity's aid?
Thy visage wan did e'er I woo?
Or at thy feet in homage bow?
    Or court thy sullen shade?

Even now, enchanted scenes abound,
Elysian glories strew the ground,
    To lure th' astonished eyes;
Now horrors, hell, and furies reign,
And desolate the fairy scene
    Of all its gay disguise.

The Passions, at thy urgent call,
Our Reason and our Sense enthral
    In Frenzy's fetters strong.
And now Despair, with lurid eye,
Doth meagre Poverty descry,
    Subdued by famine long.

The lover flies the haunts of day,
In gloomy woods and wilds to stray:
    There shuns his Jessy's scorn.

Sad sisters of the sighing grove
Attune their lyres to hapless love,
     Dejected and forlorn.

Yet Hope, undaunted, wears thy chain,
And smiles amidst the growing pain,
     Nor fears thy sad dismay;
Unaw'd by Power, her fancy flies
From earth's dim orb to purer skies,
     To realms of endless day.

SONG.

WHERE winding Forth adorns the vale,
   Fond Strephon, once a shepherd gay,
Did to the rocks his lot bewail,
   And thus addressed his plaintive lay:
" O Julia! more than lily fair,
   " More blooming than the budding rose,
" How can thy breast, relentless, bear
   " A heart more cold than Winter's snows.

" Yet nipping Winter's keenest sway,
   " But for a short-liv'd space prevails:
" Spring soon returns, and cheers each spray,
   " Scented with Flora's fragrant gales.

" Come, Julia! come; thy love obey,
  " Thou mistress of angelic charms!
" Come, smiling like the morn in May,
  " And bless thy Strephon's longing arms:

" Else, haunted by the fiend Despair,
  " He'll court some solitary grove,
" Where mortal foot did ne'er repair,
  " But swains oppressed by hapless love.
" From the once pleasing rural throng
  " Removed, he'll thro' the desert stray,
" Where Philomela's mournful song
  " Shall join his melancholy lay."

═══

SONG.

Amidst a rosy bank of flowers,
  Damon, forlorn, deplored his fate;
In sighs he spent his languid hours,
  And breathed his woes in doleful state.

Gay joy no more shall cheer his mind;
  No wanton sports can soothe his care;
Since sweet Amanda prov'd unkind,
  And left him full of black despair.

His looks, that were as fresh as morn,
   Can now no longer smiles impart;
His pensive soul, on sadness borne,
   Is rack'd and torn by Cupid's dart.

Turn, fair Amanda! cheer your swain;
   Unshroud him from his veil of woe;
Turn, gentle nymph! and ease the pain
   That in his tortured breast doth grow.

===

SONG.

Since brightest beauty soon must fade,
   That in life's Spring so long has rolled,
And wither in the drooping shade,
   Ere it return to native mould:

Ye virgins! seize the fleeting hour,
   In time catch Cytherea's joy,
Ere age your wonted smiles deflower,
   And hopes of love and life annoy.

PASTORAL I.—*Morning.*

DAMON—ALEXIS.

DAMON.

Aurora now her welcome visit pays ;
Stern Darkness flies before her cheerful rays ;
Cool circling breezes whirl along the air,
And early shepherds to the fields repair :
Lead we our flocks, then, to the mountain's
      brow,
Where junipers and thorny brambles grow ;
Where founts of water 'midst the daisies spring,
And soaring larks and tuneful linnets sing ;
Your pleasing song shall teach our flocks to
      stray,
While sounding echoes smooth the sylvan lay.

ALEXIS.

'Tis thine to sing the graces of the morn,
The zephyr trembling o'er the rip'ning corn ;

'Tis thine with ease to chant the rural lay,
While bubbling fountains to your numbers play.
No piping swain that treads the verdant field,
But to your music and your verse must yield:
Sing then,—for here we may with safety keep
Our sportive lambkins on this mossy steep.

DAMON.

With ruddy glow the sun adorns the land,
The pearly dew-drops on the bushes stand ;
The lowing oxen from the folds we hear,
And snowy flocks upon the hills appear.

ALEXIS.

How sweet the murmurs of the neighbouring
    rill !
Sweet are the slumbers which its floods distill !
Thro' pebbly channels winding as they run,
And brilliant sparkling to the rising sun.

DAMON.

Behold Edina's lofty turrets rise !
Her structures fair adorn the eastern skies :
As Pentland's cliffs o'ertop yon distant plain,
So she the cities on our north domain.

ALEXIS.

Boast not of cities, or their lofty tow'rs,
Where Discord all her baneful influence pours ;

The homely cottage, and the withered tree,
With sweet Content, shall be preferred by me.

DAMON.

The hemlock dire shall please the heifer's
    taste,
Our lands like wild Arabia be waste,
The bee forget to range for winter's food,
Ere I forsake the forest and the flood.

ALEXIS.

Ye balmy breezes! wave the verdant field;
Clouds! all your bounties, all your moisture
    yield;
That fruits and herbage may our farms adorn,
And furrow'd ridges teem with loaded corn.

DAMON.

The year already has propitious smiled;
Gentle in spring-time, and in summer mild;
No cutting blasts have hurt my tender dams;
No hoary frosts destroyed my infant lambs.

ALEXIS.

If Ceres crown with joy the bounteous year,
A sacred altar to her shrine I'll rear;
A vigorous ram shall bleed, whose curling horns
His woolly neck and hardy front adorns.

DAMON.

Teach me, O Pan! to tune the slender reed,
No favourite ram shall at thine altars bleed ;
Each breathing morn thy woodland verse I'll
    sing,
And hollow dens shall with the numbers ring.

ALEXIS.

Apollo ! lend me thy celestial lyre,
The woods in concert join at thy desire :
At morn, at noon, at night, I'll tune the lay,
And bid fleet Echo bear the sound away.

DAMON.

Sweet are the breezes, when cool eve returns,
To lowing herds, when raging Syrius burns :
Not half so sweetly winds the breeze along,
As does the murmur of your pleasing song.

ALEXIS.

To hear your strains the cattle spurn their food;
The feathered songsters leave their tender brood;
Around your seat the silent lambs advance ;
And scrambling he-goats on the mountains dance.

DAMON.

But haste, Alexis, reach yon leafy shade,
Which mantling ivy round the oaks hath made ;

There we'll retire, and list the warbling note
That flows melodious from the blackbird's
　　throat;
Your easy numbers shall his songs inspire,
And every warbler join the general choir.

———

PASTORAL II.—*Noon.*

CORYDON—TIMANTHES.

CORYDON.

THE sun the summit of his orb hath gained;
No fleckered clouds his azure path hath stained;
Our pregnant ewes around us cease to graze,
Stung with the keenness of his sultry rays;
The weary bullock from the yoke is led,
And youthful shepherds from the plains are fled
To dusky shades, where scarce a glimmering
　　ray
Can dart its lustre thro' the leafy spray.
Yon cooling rivulet where the waters gleam,
Where springing flowers adorn the limpid
　　stream,
Invites us where the drooping willow grows,
To guide our flocks, and take a cool repose.

TIMANTHES.

To thy advice a grateful ear I'll lend;
The shades I'll court where slender osiers bend;
Our weanlings young shall crop the rising flower,
While we retire to yonder twining bower;
The woods shall echo back thy cheerful strains,
Admired by all our Caledonian swains.

CORYDON.

There have I oft with gentle Delia strayed,
Amidst th' embowering solitary shade,
Before the gods to thwart my wishes strove,
By blasting every pleasing glimpse of love:
For Delia wanders o'er the Anglian plains,
Where civil Discord and sedition reigns.
There Scotia's sons in odious light appear,
Tho' we for them have waved the hostile spear.
For them my sire, enwrapped in curdled gore,
Breathed his last moments on a foreign shore.

TIMANTHES.

Six lunar months, my friend, will soon expire,
And she return to crown your fond desire.
For her, oh rack not your desponding mind!
In Delia's breast a generous flame's confined,
That burns for Corydon, whose piping lay
Has caused the tedious moments steal away;

Whose strains melodious moved the falling floods
To whisper Delia to the rising woods.
Oh ! if your sighs could aid the floating gales,
That favourable swell their lofty sails,
Ne'er should your sobs their rapid flight give
     o'er,
Till Delia's presence graced our northern shore!

CORYDON.

Tho' Delia greet my love, I sigh in vain ;
Such joy unbounded can I ne'er obtain.
Her sire a thousand fleeces numbers o'er,
And grassy hills increase the milky store ;
While the weak fences of a scanty fold
Will all my sheep and fattening lambkins hold.

TIMANTHES.

Ah, hapless youth ! altho' the early Muse
Painted her semblance on thy youthful brows ;
Tho' she with laurels twined thy temples round,
And in thy ear distilled the magic sound ;
A cheerless poverty attends thy woes ;
Your song melodious unrewarded flows.

CORYDON.

Think not, Timanthes, that for wealth I pine,
Tho' all the fates to make me poor combine :
Tay, bounding o'er its banks with awful sway,
Bore all my corns and all my flocks away.

Of Jove's dread precepts did I e'er complain?
E'er curse the rapid flood, or dashing rain?
Ev'n now I sigh not for my former store,
But wish the gods had destined Delia poor.

TIMANTHES.

'Tis joy, my friend, to think I can repay
The loss you bore by Autumn's rigid sway.
Yon fertile meadow where the daisies spring,
Shall yearly pasture to your heifers bring:
Your flock with mine shall on yon mountain
    feed,
Cheered by the warbling of your tuneful reed:
No more shall Delia's ever-fretful sire
Against your hopes and ardent love conspire.
Roused by her smiles, you'll tune the happy lay,
While hills responsive waft your songs away.

CORYDON.

May plenteous crops your irksome labour
    crown;
May hoodwinked Fortune cease her envious
    frown;
May riches still increase with growing years;
Your flocks be numerous as your silver hairs.

TIMANTHES.

But, lo! the heats invite us at our ease,
To court the twining shades and cooling breeze;

Our languid joints we'll peaceably recline,
And 'midst the flowers and opening blossoms
    dine.

===

PASTORAL III.—*Night.*

AMYNTAS—FLORELLUS.

AMYNTAS.

WHILE yet grey Twilight does his empire hold,
Drive all our heifers to the peaceful fold.
With sullied wing grim Darkness soars along,
And larks to nightingales resign the song :
The weary ploughman flies the waving fields,
To taste what fare his humble cottage yields ;
As bees, that daily thro' the meadows roam,
Feed on the sweets they have prepared at home.

FLORELLUS.

The grassy meads that smiled serenely gay,
Cheered by the ever-burning lamp of day,
In dusky hue attired, are cramped with colds,
And springing flowerets shut their crimson folds.

AMYNTAS.

What awful silence reigns thro'out the shade!
The peaceful olive bends his drooping head;
No sound is heard o'er all the gloomy maze;
Wide o'er the deep the fiery meteors blaze.

FLORELLUS.

The west, yet tinged with Sol's effulgent ray,
With feeble light illumes our homeward way;
The glowing stars with keener lustre burn,
While round the earth their glowing axles turn.

AMYNTAS.

What mighty power conducts the stars on high!
Who bids these comets thro' our system fly!
Who wafts the lightning to the icy pole,
And thro' our regions bids the thunders roll?

FLORELLUS.

But say, what mightier power from nought
        could raise
The earth, the sun, and all that fiery maze
Of distant stars that gild the azure sky,
And thro' the void in settled orbits fly?

AMYNTAS.

That righteous Power, before whose heavenly eye
The stars are nothing, and the planets die;

Whose breath divine supports our mortal
      frame;
Who made the lion wild and lambkin tame.

FLORELLUS.

At His command the bounteous Spring re-
      turns;
Hot Summer, raging o'er th' Atlantic, burns;
The yellow Autumn crowns our sultry toil;
And Winter's snows prepare the cumbrous soil.

AMYNTAS.

By Him the morning darts his purple ray;
To Him the birds their early homage pay;
With vocal harmony the meadows ring,
While swains in concert heavenly praises sing.

FLORELLUS.

Swayed by his word, the nutrient dews descend,
And growing pastures to the moisture bend;
The vernal blossoms sip his falling showers;
The meads are garnished with his opening flowers.

AMYNTAS.

For man, the object of his chiefest care,
Fowls he hath formed to wing the ambient air:
For him the steer his lusty neck doth bend;
Fishes for him their scaly fins extend.

FLORELLUS.

Wide o'er the orient sky the moon appears,
A foe to Darkness and his idle fears ;
Around her orb the stars in clusters shine,
And distant planets 'tend her silver shrine.

AMYNTAS.

Hushed are the busy numbers of the day ;
On downy couch they sleep their hours away.
Hail, balmy sleep, that sooths the troubled
    mind !
Locked in thy arms, our cares a refuge find.
Oft do you tempt us with delusive dreams,
When wildering Fancy darts her dazzling
    beams.
Asleep, the lover with his mistress strays
Thro' lonely thickets and untrodden ways ;
But when pale Cynthia's sable empire's fled,
And hovering slumbers shun the morning bed,
Roused by the dawn, he wakes with frequent
    sigh,
And all his flattering visions quickly fly.

FLORELLUS.

Now owls and bats infest the midnight scene ;
Dire snakes envenomed twine along the green ;
Forsook by man the rivers mourning glide,
And groaning echoes swell the noisy tide ;

Straight to our cottage let us bend our way ;
My drowsy powers confess sleep's magic sway.
Easy and calm upon our couch we'll lie,
While sweet reviving slumbers round our pil-
lows fly.

THE SIMILE.

AT noontide, as Colin and Sylvia lay
   Within a cool jessamin bower,
A butterfly, waked by the heat of the day,
   Was sipping the juice of each flow'r.

Near the shade of this covert a young shep-
     herd boy
   The gaudy brisk flutterer spies,
Who held it as pastime to seek and destroy
   Each beautiful insect that flies.

From the lily he hunted this fly to the rose ;
   From the rose to the lily again ;
Till, weary with tracing its motions, he chose
   To leave the pursuit with disdain.

Then Colin to Sylvia smilingly said,
   Amyntor has followed you long ;
From him, like the butterfly, still have you
      fled,
   Tho' wooed by his musical tongue.

Beware in persisting to start from his arms,
   But with his fond wishes comply ;
Come, take my advice ; or he's palled with
      your charms,
   Like the youth and the beautiful fly.

Says Sylvia,—Colin, thy simile's just,
   But still to Amyntor I'm coy ;
For I vow she's a simpleton blind that would
      trust
   A swain, when he courts to destroy.

====

THE COMPLAINT.

NEAR the heart of a fair-spreading grove,
   Whose foliage shaded the green,
A shepherd, repining at love,
   In anguish was heard to complain.—

" O Cupid ! thou wanton young boy !
" Since, with thy invisible dart,
" Thou hast robbed a fond youth of his joy,
" In return grant the wish of his heart.

" Send a shaft so severe from thy bow,
" (His pining, his sighs, to remove),
" That Stella, once wounded, may know
" How keen are the arrows of love.

" No swain once so happy as I,
" Nor tuned with more pleasure the reed ;
" My breast never vented a sigh,
" Till Stella approached the gay mead.

" With mirth, with contentment endowed,
" My hours they flew wantonly by ;
" I sought no repose in the wood,
" Nor from my few sheep would I fly.

" Now my reed I have carelessly broke ;
" It's melody pleases no more :
" I pay no regard to a flock
" That seldom hath wandered before.

" O Stella ! whose beauty so fair
" Excels the bright splendor of day,
" Ah ! have you no pity to share
" With Damon thus fallen to decay ?

" For you have I quitted the plain;
 " Forsaken my sheep and my fold:
" To you in dull languor and pain
 " My tedious moments are told.

" For you have my roses grown pale;
 " They have faded untimely away:
" And will not such beauty bewail
 " A shepherd thus fallen to decay?

" Since your eyes still requite me with scorn,
 " And kill with their merciless ray;
" Like a star at the dawning of morn,
 " I fall to their lustre a prey.

" Some swain who shall mournfully go
 " To whisper love's sigh to the shade,
" Will haply some charity shew,
 " And under the turf see me laid.

" Would my love but in pity appear
 " On the spot where he moulds my cold grave,
" And bedew the green sod with a tear,
 " 'Tis all the remembrance I crave."

To the sward then his visage he turned;
 'Twas wan as the lilies in May:
Fair Stella may see him inurned;
 He hath sighed all his sorrows away.

RETIREMENT.

Come, Inspiration! from thy vernal bow'r,
    To thy celestial voice attune the lyre;
Smooth gliding strains in sweet profusion pour,
    And aid my numbers with seraphic fire.

Under a lonely spreading oak I lay,
    My head upon the daisied green reclined;
The evening sun beamed forth his parting ray;
    The foliage bended to the hollow wind.

There gentle Sleep my acting powers supprest;
    The city's distant hum was heard no more;
Yet Fancy suffered not the mind to rest,
    Ever obedient to her wakeful power.

She led me near a crystal fountain's noise,
    Where undulating waters sportive play;
Where a young comely swain, with pleasing
        voice,
    In tender accents sung his sylvan lay.

" Adieu, ye baneful pleasures of the town !
  " Farewel, ye giddy and unthinking throng!
" Without regret your foibles I disown ;
  " Themes more exalted claim the Muse's
    " song.

" Your stony hearts no social feelings share ;
  " Your souls of distant sorrows ne'er partake;
" Ne'er do you listen to the needy prayer,
  " Nor drop a tear for tender pity's sake.

" Welcome, ye fields, ye fountains, and ye
    " groves !
  " Ye flowery meadows, and extensive plains!
" Where soaring warblers pour their plaintive
    " loves,
  " Each landscape cheering with their vocal
    " strains.

" Here rural Beauty rears her pleasing shrine;
  " She on the margin of each streamlet
    " glows ;
" Where with the blooming hawthorn roses
    " twine,
  " And the fair lily of the valley grows.

" Here Chastity may wander unassailed,
  " Thro' fields where gay seducers cease to
    " rove ;

" Where open Vice o'er Virtue ne'er pre-
" vailed ;
" Where all is innocence, and all is love.

" Peace with her olive wand triumphant reigns,
" Guarding secure the peasant's humble
" bed ;
" Envy is banished from the happy plains,
" And Defamation's busy tongue is laid.

" Health and Contentment usher in the morn ;
" With jocund smiles they cheer the rural
" swain ;
" For which the peer, to pompous titles born,
" Forsaken sighs, but all his sighs are vain.

" For the calm comforts of an easy mind,
" In yonder lonely cot delight to dwell,
" And leave the statesman for the labouring
" hind,
" The regal palace for the lowly cell.

" Ye, who to Wisdom would devote your
" hours,
" And far from riot, far from discord stray !
" Look back disdainful on the city's towers,
" Where Pride, where Folly, point the slip-
" pery way.

" Pure flows the limpid stream in crystal tides,
 " Thro' rocks, thro' dens. and ever-verdant
  " vales,
" Till to the town's unhallowed wall it glides,
 " Where all its purity and lustre fails."

ON THE

COLD MONTH OF APRIL, 1771,

Oh ! who can hold a fire in his hand
By thinking on the frosty Caucasus ;
Or cloy the hungry edge of appetite
By bare imagination of a feast ;
Or wallow naked in December's snow
By thinking on fantastic Summer's heat ?

    Shakesp. Richard II.

Poets in vain have hailed the opening Spring,
 In tender accents wooed the blooming maid,
In vain have taught the April birds to wing
 Their flight thro' fields in verdant hue array'd.

The Muse, in every season taught to sing
  Amidst the desert snows, by Fancy's powers,
Can elevated soar, on placid wing,
  To climes where Spring her kindest influ-
    ence showers.

April! once famous for the zephyr mild;
  For sweets that early in the garden grow;
Say, how converted to this cheerless wild,
  Rushing with torrents of dissolving snow.

Nursed by the moisture of a gentle shower,
  Thy foliage oft hath sounded to the breeze;
Oft did thy choristers melodious pour
  Their melting numbers thro' the shady trees.

Fair have I seen thy morn, in smiles arrayed,
  With crimson blush bepaint the eastern sky;
But now the dawn creeps mournful o'er the
    glade,
  Shrowded in colours of a sable dye.

So have I seen the fair, with laughing eye,
  And visage cheerful as the smiling morn,
Alternate changing for the heaving sigh,
  Or frowning aspect of contemptuous scorn.

Life! what art thou?—a variegated scene
  Of mingled light and shade, of joy and woe;

A sea where calms and storms promiscuous
    reign ;
A stream where sweet and bitter jointly flow.

Mute are the plains; the shepherd pipes no
    more ;
    The reed's forsaken, and the tender flock ;
While Echo, listening to the tempest's roar,
    In silence wanders o'er the beetling rock.

Winter, too potent for the solar ray,
    Bestrides the blast, ascends his icy throne,
And views Britannia, subject to his sway,
    Floating emergent on the frigid zone.

Thou savage tyrant of the fretful sky !
    Wilt thou for ever in our zenith reign ?
To Greenland's seas, congealed in chillness, fly,
    Where howling monsters tread the bleak do-
    main.

Relent, O Boreas ! leave thy frozen cell ;
    Resign to Spring her portion of the year ;
Let west winds temp'rate wave the flowing gale,
    And hills, and vales, and woods, a vernal
    aspect wear.

VERSES

Written at the Hermitage of Braid, near Edinburgh.

WOULD you relish a rural retreat,
　Or the pleasure the groves can inspire ?
The city's allurements forget,—
　To this spot of enchantment retire ;

Where a valley and crystalline brook,
　Whose current glides sweetly along,
Give Nature a fanciful look,
　The beautiful woodlands among.

Behold the umbrageous trees
　A covert of verdure have spread,
Where shepherds may loll at their ease,
　And pipe to the musical shade.

For, lo ! thro' each op'ning is heard,
　In concert with waters below,
The voice of a musical bird,
　Whose numbers melodiously flow.

The bushes and arbours so green,
  The tendrils of spray interwove,
With foliage shelter the scene,
  And form a retirement for love.

Here Venus, transported, may rove
  From pleasure to pleasure unseen,
Nor wish for the Cyprian grove
  Her youthful Adonis to screen.

Oft let me contemplative dwell
  On a scene where such beauties appear :—
I could live in a cot or a cell,
  And never think solitude near.

DAMON TO HIS FRIENDS.

The billows of life are supprest ;
  Its tumults, its toils disappear ;
To relinquish the storms that are past,
  I think on the sunshine that's near.

Dame Fortune and I are agreed ;
  Her frowns I no longer endure ;

For the goddess has kindly decreed,
  That Damon no more shall be poor.

Now riches will ope the dim eyes,
  To view the increase of my store;
And many my friendship will prize,
  Who never knew Damon before.

But those I renounce and abjure,
  Who carried contempt in their eye;
May poverty still be their dower,
  That could look on misfortune awry!

Ye powers that weak mortals govern,
  Keep Pride at his bay from my mind;
O let me not haughtily learn
  To despise the few friends that were kind.

For their's was a feeling sincere;
  'Twas free from delusion and art;
O may I that friendship revere,
  And hold it yet dear to my heart!

By which was I ever forgot?
  It was both my physician and cure,
That still found the way to my cot,
  Altho' I was wretched and poor.

'Twas balm to my canker-toothed care;
   The wound of affliction it healed:
In distress it was Pity's soft tear,
   And naked cold Poverty's shield.

Attend, ye kind youth of the plain!
   Who oft with my sorrows condoled;
You cannot be deaf to the strain,
   Since Damon is master of gold.

I have chose a sweet sylvan retreat,
   Bedecked with the beauties of Spring;
Around, my flocks nibble and bleat,
   While the musical choristers sing.

I force not the waters to stand
   In an artful canal at my door;
But a river, at Nature's command,
   Meanders both limpid and pure.

She's the goddess that darkens my bowers
   With tendrils of ivy and vine;
She tutors my shrubs and my flowers;
   Her taste is the standard of mine.

What a pleasing diversified group
   Of trees has she spread o'er my ground!
She has taught the grave lyrax to droop,
   And the birch to shed odours around.

For whom has she perfumed my groves?
  For whom has she clustered my vine?
If Friendship despise my alcoves,
  They'll ne'er be recesses of mine.

He who tastes his grape juices by stealth,
  Without chosen companions to share,
Is the basest of slaves to his wealth,
  And the pitiful minion of care.

O come, and with Damon retire
  Amidst the green umbrage embowered!
Your mirth and your songs to inspire,
  Shall the juice of his vintage be poured.

O come, ye dear friends of his youth!
  Of all his good fortune partake!
Nor think 'tis departing from truth,
  To say 'twas preserved for your sake.

CONSCIENCE.

———Leave her to Heaven,
And to the thorns that in her bosom lodge,
To prick and sting her.

SHAKESP.

No choiring warblers flutter in the sky;
Phœbus no longer holds his radiant sway;
While Nature, with a melancholy eye,
Bemoans the loss of his departed ray.

O happy he, whose conscience knows no guile!
He to the sable night can bid farewel;
From cheerless objects close his eyes a while,
Within the silken folds of sleep to dwell.

Elysian dreams shall hover round his bed;
His soul shall wing, on pleasing fancies borne,
To shining vales where flowerets lift their head,
Waked by the breathing zephyrs of the morn.

But wretched he, whose foul reproachful deeds
   Can thro' an angry conscience wound his
      rest;
His eye too oft the balmy comfort needs,
   Tho' Slumber seldom knows him as her
      guest.

To calm the raging tumults of his soul,
   If wearied Nature should an hour demand,
Around his bed the sheeted spectres howl; .
   Red with revenge the grinning furies stand.

Nor state nor grandeur can his pain allay;
   Where shall he find a requiem to his woes;
Power cannot chase the frightful gloom away,
   Nor music lull him to a kind repose.

Where is the king that Conscience fears to
      chide?—
   Conscience, that candid judge of right and
      wrong,
Will o'er the secrets of each heart preside,
   Nor awed by pomp, nor tamed by soothing
      song.

AGAINST REPINING AT FORTUNE.

Tho' in my narrow bounds of rural toil,
   No obelisk or splendid column rise;
Tho' partial Fortune still averts her smile,
   And views my labours with condemning eyes;

Yet all the gorgeous vanity of state
   I can contemplate with a cool disdain;
Nor shall the honours of the gay and great
   E'er wound my bosom with an envious pain.

Avails it aught the grandeur of their halls,
   With all the glories of the pencil hung,
If Truth, fair Truth! within the unhallowed
     walls,
   Hath never whispered with her seraph tongue?

Avails it aught, if Music's gentle lay
   Hath oft been echoed by the sounding dome,
If Music cannot sooth their griefs away,
   Or change a wretched to a happy home?

Tho' Fortune should invest them with her spoils,
 And banish Poverty with look severe,—
Enlarge their confines, and decrease their toils,
 Ah ! what avails, if she increase their care?

Tho' fickle, she disclaim my moss-grown cot,
 Nature ! thou lookest with more impartial
   eyes :
Smile thou, fair goddess ! on my sober lot ;
 I'll neither fear her fall, nor court her rise.

When early larks shall cease the matin-song ;
 When Philomel at night resigns her lays ;
When melting numbers to the owl belong :
 Then shall the reed be silent in thy praise.

Can he, who with the tide of Fortune sails,
 More pleasure from the sweets of Nature
   share ?
Do zephyrs waft him more ambrosial gales,
 Or do his groves a gayer livery wear ?

To me the heavens unveil as pure a sky ;
 To me the flowers as rich a bloom disclose ;
The morning beams as radiant to mine eye ;
 And darkness guides me to as sweet repose.

If luxury their lavish dainties piles,
 And still attends upon their sated hours,

Doth Health reward them with her open smiles,
    Or Exercise enlarge their feeble powers?

'Tis not in richest mines of Indian gold,
    That man this jewel, HAPPINESS, can find,
If his unfeeling breast, to Virtue cold,
    Denies her entrance to his ruthless mind.

Wealth, pomp, and honour, are but gaudy
        toys;
    Alas! how poor the pleasures they impart!
Virtue's the sacred source of all the joys
    That claim a lasting mansion in the heart.

THE DECAY OF FRIENDSHIP,

A PASTORAL ELEGY.

WHEN Gold, man's sacred deity, did smile,
    My friends were plenty, and my sorrows few;
Mirth, love, and bumpers, did my hours be-
        guile,
    And arrowed Cupids round my slumbers flew.

What shepherd then could boast more happy
  days ?
My lot was envied by each humbler swain ;
Each bard in smooth eulogium sung my praise,
  And Damon listened to the guileful strain.

Flattery ! alluring as the Syren's lay,
  And as deceitful thy enchanting tongue,
How have you taught my wavering mind to stray,
  Charmed and attracted by the baneful song?

My pleasant cottage, sheltered from the gale,
  Arose, with moss and rural ivy bound ;
And scarce a floweret in my lowly vale,
  But was with bees of various colours crowned.

Free o'er my lands the neighbouring flocks could
  roam ;
  How welcome were the swains and flocks to
  me !
The shepherds kindly were invited home,
  To chase the hours in merriment and glee.

To wake emotions in the youthful mind,
  Strephon, with voice melodious, tuned the
  song ;
Each sylvan youth the sounding chorus joined,
  Fraught with contentment 'midst the festive
  throng.

My clustering grape compens'd their magic
    skill;
The bowl capacious swelled, in purple tide,
To shepherds, liberal as the crystal rill
    Spontaneous gurgling from the mountain's
    side.

But, ah! these youthful sportive hours are fled;
    These scenes of jocund mirth are now no
    more:
No healing slumbers 'tend my humble bed;
    No friends condole the sorrows of the poor.

And what avail the thoughts of former joy?
    What comfort bring they in the adverse
    hour?
Can they the canker-worm of Care destroy,
    Or brighten Fortune's discontented lour?

He who hath long traversed the fertile plain,
    Where Nature in its fairest vesture smiled,
Will he not cheerless view the fairy scene,
    When lonely wandering o'er the barren wild?

For now pale Poverty, with haggard eye,
    And rueful aspect, darts her gloomy ray;
My wonted guests their proffered aid deny,
    And from the paths of Damon steal away.

Thus, when fair Summer's lustre gilds the
    lawn,
  When ripening blossoms deck the spreading
    tree,
The birds with melody salute the dawn,
  And o'er the daisy hangs the humming bee:

But when the beauties of the circling year,
  In chilling frosts and furious storms decay,
No more the bees upon the plains appear;
  No more the warblers hail the infant day.

To the lone corner of some distant shore,
  In dreary devious pilgrimage I'll fly,
And wander pensive, where Deceit no more
  Shall trace my footsteps with a mortal eye:

There solitary saunter o'er the beach,
  And to the murmuring surge my griefs dis-
    close;
There shall my voice in plaintive wailings
    teach
  The hollow caverns to resound my woes.

Sweet are the waters to the parched tongue;
  Sweet are the blossoms to the wanton bee;
Sweet to the shepherd sounds the lark's shrill
    song:
  But sweeter far is SOLITUDE to me.

Adieu, ye fields, where I have fondly strayed!
 Ye swains, who once the favourite Damon
  knew!
Farewel, ye sharers of my bounty's aid!
 Ye sons of base INGRATITUDE, adieu!

TO THE MEMORY OF

JOHN CUNNINGHAM, POET.

Sing his praises that doth keep
 Our flocks from harm ;
Pan, the father of our sheep :
 And, arm in arm,
Tread we softly in a round
While the hollow neighbouring ground
Fills the music with her sound.

    BEAUMONT & FLETCHER.

YE mournful meanders and groves,
 Delight of the Muse and her song!
Ye grottos and dripping alcoves,
 No strangers to Corydon's tongue!

Let each Sylvan and Dryad declare
  His themes and his music how dear !
Their plaints and their dirges prepare,
  Attendant on Corydon's bier.

The Echo that joined in the lay,
  So amorous, sprightly, and free,
Shall send forth the sounds of dismay,
  And sigh with sad pity for thee.

Wild wander his flocks with the breeze ;
  His reed can no longer control ;
His numbers no longer can please,
  Or send kind relief to the soul.

But long may they wander and bleat ;
  To hills tell the tale of their woe ;
The woodlands the tale shall repeat,
  And the waters shall mournfully flow.

For these were the haunts of his love,
  The sacred retreats of his ease,
Where favourite Fancy would rove,
  As wanton, as light as the breeze.

Her zone will discoloured appear,
  With fanciful ringlets unbound ;
A face pale and languid she'll wear ;
  A heart fraught with sorrow profound.

The reed of each shepherd will mourn;
  The shades of Parnassus decay:
The Muses will dry their sad urn,
  Since 'reft of young Corydon's lay.

To him every passion was known
  That throbbed in the breast with desire;
Each gentle affection was shewn
  In the soft-sighing songs of his lyre.

Like the caroling thrush on the spray,
  In music soft warbling and wild,
To love was devoted each lay,
  In accents pathetic and mild.

Let Beauty and Virtue revere,
  And the songs of the shepherd approve,
Who felt, who lamented the snare,
  When repining at pitiless love.

The Summer but languidly gleams;
  Pomona no comfort can bring;
Nor valleys, nor grottos, nor streams,
  Nor the May-born flowerets of Spring.

They've fled all with Corydon's Muse,
  For his brows to form chaplets of woe;
Whose reed oft awakened their boughs,
  As the whispering breezes that blow.

To many a fanciful spring
  His lyre was melodiously strung ;
While fairies and fawns, in a ring,
  Have applauded the swain as he sung.

To the cheerful he ushered his smiles ;
  To the woeful his sigh and his tear ;
A condoler with Want and her toils,
  When the voice of Oppression was near.

Tho' titles and wealth were his due ;
  Tho' Fortune denied his reward ;
Yet Truth and Sincerity knew
  What the goddess would never regard.

Avails aught the generous heart,
  Which Nature to Goodness designed,
If Fortune denies to impart
  Her kindly relief to the mind ?

'Twas but faint the relief to dismay,
  The cells of the wretched among ;
Tho' Sympathy sung in the lay ;
  Tho' melody fell from his tongue.

Let the favoured of Fortune attend
  To the ails of the wretched and poor :
Tho' Corydon's lays could befriend,
  'Tis riches alone that can cure.

But they to Compassion are dumb ;
  To Pity their voices unknown ;
Near Sorrow they never can come,
  Till Misfortune has marked them her own.

Now the shades of the evening depend ;
  Each warbler is lulled on the spray ;
The cypress doth ruefully bend
  Where reposes the Shepherd's cold clay.

Adieu, then, the songs of the swain:
  Let Peace still attend on his shade ;
And his pipe, that is dumb to his strain,
  In the grave be with Corydon laid.

THE DELIGHTS OF VIRTUE.

RETURNING morn, in orient blush arrayed,
  With gentle radiance hailed the sky serene ;
No rustling breezes waved the verdant shade ;
  No swelling surge disturbed the azure main.

These moments, MEDITATION ! sure are thine ;
  These are the halcyon joys you wish to find,

When Nature's peaceful elements combine
  To suit the calm composure of the mind.

The Muse, exalted by thy sacred power,
  To the green mountain's airy summit flew,
Charmed with the thoughtful stilness of an
      hour,
  That ushered beaming Fancy to her view.

Fresh from old Neptune's fluid mansion sprung
  The Sun, reviver of each drooping flower ;
At his approach, the lark, with matin song,
  In notes of gratitude confessed his power.

So shines fair Virtue, shedding light divine
  On those who wish to profit by her ways ;
Who ne'er at parting with their vice repine,
  To taste the comforts of her blissful rays.

She, with fresh hopes each sorrow can beguile,
  Can dissipate Adversity's deep gloom,
Make meagre Poverty contented smile,
  And the sad wretch forget his hapless doom.

Sweeter than shady groves in Summer's pride,
  Than flowery dales or grassy meads, is she ;
Delightful as the honeyed streams that glide
  From the rich labours of the busy bee.

Her paths and alleys are for ever green :—
　　There Innocence, in snowy robes arrayed,
With smiles of pure content, is hailed the
　　　　queen
　　And happy mistress of the sacred shade.

O let no transient gleam of earthly joy
　　From virtue lure your labouring steps aside ;
Nor instant grandeur future hopes annoy
　　With thoughts that spring from insolence
　　　　and pride.

Soon will the winged moments speed away,
　　When you'll no more the plumes of honour
　　　　wear :
Grandeur must shudder at the sad decay,
　　And Pride look humble when he ponders
　　　　there.

Deprived of Virtue, where is Beauty's power ?
　　Her dimpled smiles, her roses, charm no
　　　　more.
So much can guilt the loveliest form deflower:—
　　We loathe that beauty which we loved before.

How fair are Virtue's buds, where'er they blow,
　　Or in the desert wild, or garden gay !
Her flowers how sacred, wheresoe'er they shew,
　　Unknown to killing canker and decay !

DIRGE.

THE waving yew or cypress wreath
  In vain bequeath the mighty tear ;
In vain the awful pomp of Death
  Attends the sable-shrouded bier.

Since Strephon's virtue's sunk to rest,
  Nor Pity's sigh, nor Sorrow's strain,
Nor magic tongue, have e'er confest
  Our wounded bosom's secret pain.

The just, the good, more honours share
  In what the conscious heart bestows,
Than Vice adorned with sculptor's care,
  In all the venal pomp of woes.

A sad-eyed mourner at his tomb,
  Thou, Friendship ! pay thy rites divine,
And echo thro' the midnight gloom
  That Strephon's early fall was thine.

=

ON NIGHT.

Now murky shades surround the pole :
Darkness lords without control ;
To the notes of buzzing owl,
Lions roar, and tygers howl,
Fright'ning from their azure shrine,
Stars that wont in orbs to shine :
Now the sailor's storm-tost bark
Knows no blest celestial mark,
While in the briny-troubled deep,
Dolphins change their sport for sleep :
Ghosts and frightful spectres gaunt,
Church-yards dreary footsteps haunt,
And brush with withered arms the dews
That fall upon the drooping yews.

A TALE.

THOSE rigid pedagogues and fools,
Who walk by self-invented rules,
Do often try, with empty head,
The emptier mortals to mislead,
And fain would urge that none but they
Could rightly teach the A, B, C ;
On which they've got an endless comment,
To trifling minds of mighty moment,
Throwing such barriers in the way
Of those who genius display,
As often, ah ! too often teaze
Them out of patience, and of fees,
Before they're able to explode
Obstructions thrown on Learning's road.
May mankind all employ their tools
To banish pedantry from schools !
And may each pedagogue avail,
By listening to the after tale !

Wise Mr Birch had long intended
The alphabet should be amended,
And taught that H a breathing was ;
Ergo he saw no proper cause
Why such a letter should exist.
Thus in a breath was he dismissed,
With, " O beware, beware, O youth !
" Take not the villain in your mouth."
   One day this alphabetic sinner
Was eager to devour his dinner,
When, to appease the craving glutton,
His boy Tom produced the mutton.
Was such disaster ever told ?
Alas, the meat was deadly cold !
Here take and h—eat it, says the master ;
Quoth Tom, that shall be done, and fast, Sir :
And few there are who will dispute it,
But he went instantly about it ;
For Birch had scorned the H to say,
And blew him with a puff away.
   The bell was rung with dread alarm.—
" Bring me the mutton :—Is it warm ?"
' Sir, you desired, and I have eat it.'
" You lie, my orders were to heat it."
Quoth Tom, I'll readily allow
That H is but a breathing now.

143

=

EXTEMPORE,

On being asked, Which of Three Sisters was the most beautiful?

WHEN Paris gave his voice, in Ida's grove,
For the resistless Venus, queen of love,
'Twas no great task to pass a judgment there,
Where she alone was exquisitely fair:
But here, what could his ablest judgment teach,
When wisdom, power, and beauty, reign in
    each?
The youth, non-plused, behoved to join with
    me,
And wish the apple had been cut in three.

THE

TOWN and COUNTRY CONTRASTED;

In an Epistle to a Friend.

FROM noisy bustle, from contention free,
Far from the busy town I careless loll:
Not like swain Tityrus, or the bards of old,
Under a beechen, venerable shade,
But on a furzy heath, where blooming broom
And thorny whins the spacious plains adorn.
Here Health sits smiling on my youthful brow:
For ere the sun beams forth his earliest ray,
And all the east with yellow radiance crowns;
Ere dame Aurora, from her purple bed,
'Gins with her kindling blush to paint the sky;
The soaring lark, morn's cheerful harbinger,
And linnet joyful, fluttering from the bush,
Stretch their small throats in vocal melody,
To hail the dawn, and drowsy sleep exhale
From man, frail man! on downy softness
    stretched.

Such pleasing scenes Edina cannot boast;
For there the slothful slumber sealed mine eyes,
Till nine successive strokes the clock had
knelled.
There not the lark, but fishwives' noisy screams,
And inundations plunged from ten house height,
With smell more fragrant than the spicy groves
Of Indus, fraught with all her orient stores,
Roused me from sleep;—not sweet refreshing
sleep,
But sleep infested with the burning sting
Of bug infernal, who the live-long night
With direst suction sipped my liquid gore.
There gloomy vapours in our zenith reigned,
And filled with irksome pestilence the air.
There lingering Sickness held his feeble court,
Rejoicing in the havoc he had made;
And Death, grim Death! with all his ghastly
train,
Watched the broke slumbers of Edina's sons.

Hail! rosy Health! thou pleasing antidote
'Gainst troubling cares! all hail, these rural
fields!
Those winding rivulets, and verdant shades,
Where thou, the heaven-born goddess deign'st
to dwell!
With thee the hind, upon his simple fare,

Lives cheerful, and from Heaven no more de-
    mands.
But, ah! how vast, how terrible the change
With him who night by night in sickness pines!
Him nor his splendid equipage can please,
Nor all the pageantry the world can boast;
Nay, not the consolation of his friends
Can aught avail: his hours are anguish all;
Nor cease till envious Death hath closed the
    scene.

But, Carlos, if we court this maid celestial;
Whether we thro' meandering rivers stray,
Or 'midst the city's jarring noise remain;
Let Temperance, Health's blithe concomitant,
To our desires and appetites set bounds;
Else, cloyed at last, we surfeit every joy:
Our slackened nerves reject their wonted spring;
We reap the fruits of our unkindly lusts,
And feebly totter to the silent grave.

A SATURDAY'S EXPEDITION,

IN MOCK HEROICS.

Non mira, sed vera, canam.

At that sweet period of revolving time
When Phœbus lingers not in Thetis' lap;
When twinkling stars their feeble influence shed,
And scarcely glimmer thro' th' ethereal vault,
Till Sol again his near approach proclaims,
With ray purpureal, and the blushing form
Of fair Aurora, goddess of the dawn,
Leading the winged coursers to the pole
Of Phœbus' car:—'Twas in that season fair,
When jocund Summer did the meads array
In Flora's ripening bloom, that we prepared
To break the bond of business, and to roam
Far from Edina's jarring noise a while.

Fair smiled the wakening morn on our de-
    sign ;
And we, with joy elate, our march began
For Leith's fair port, where oft Edina's sons
The week conclude, and in carousal quaff
Port, punch, rum, brandy, and Geneva strong,
Liquors too nervous for the feeble purse.
With all convenient speed we there arrived :
Nor had we time to touch at house or hall,
Till from the boat a hollow thundering voice
Bellowed vociferous, and our ears assailed
With, " Ho ! Kinghorn, oho ! come straight
    aboard."
We failed not to obey the stern command,
Uttered with voice as dreadful as the roar
Of Polyphemus, 'midst rebounding rocks,
When overcome by sage Ulysses' wiles.

" Hoist up your sails," the angry skipper
    cries,
While fore and aft the busy sailors run,
And lose th' entangled cordage.—O'er the deep
Zephyrus blows, and hugs our lofty sails,
Which, in obedience to the powerful breeze,
Swell o'er the foaming main, and kiss the
    wave.

Now o'er the convex surface of the flood
Precipitate we fly. Our foaming prow

Divides the saline stream.   On either side
Ridges of yesty surge dilate apace ;
But from the poop the waters gently flow,
And undulation for the time decays,
In eddies smoothly floating o'er the main.

Here let the Muse in doleful numbers sing
The woeful fate of those, whose cruel stars
Have doom'd them subject to the languid
          powers
Of watery sickness.—Tho' with stomach full
Of juicy beef, of mutton in its prime,
Or all the dainties Luxury can boast,
They brave the elements,—yet the rocking
          bark,
Truly regardless of their precious food,
Converts their visage to the ghastly pale,
And makes the sea partaker of the sweets'
On which they sumptuous fared.—And this
          the cause
Why those of Scotia's sons, whose wealthy
          store
Hath blessed them with a splendid coach and
          six,
Rather incline to linger on the way,
And cross the river Forth by Stirling Bridge,
Than be subjected to the ocean's swell,
To dangerous ferries, and to sickness dire.

And now at equal distance shews the land.—
Gladly the tars the joyful task pursue
Of gathering in the freight.—Debates arise
From counterfeited halfpence.—In the hold
The seamen scrutinize, and eager peep
Thro' every corner where their watchful eye
Suspects a lurking place, or dark retreat,
To hide the timid corpse of some poor soul,
Whose scanty purse can scarce one groat afford.

At length, we, cheerful, land on Fifan shore,
Where sickness vanishes, and all the ills
Attendant on the passage of Kinghorn.
Our pallid cheeks resume their rosy hue,
And empty stomachs keenly crave supply.
With eager step we reached the friendly inn ;
Nor did we think of beating our retreat
Till every gnawing appetite was quelled.

Eastward along the Fifan coast we stray :
And here th' unwearied eye may fondly gaze
O'er all the tufted groves and pointed spires
With which the pleasant banks of Forth are
    crowned.
Sweet navigable stream ! where Commerce
    reigns,
Where Peace and jocund Plenty smiles serene.
On thy green banks sits Liberty enthroned :
But not that shadow which the English youth

So eagerly pursue; but freedom bought,
When Caledonia's triumphant sword
Taught the proud sons of Anglia to bemoan
Their fate at Bannockburn, where thousands
      came,
Never to tread their native soil again.

Far in a rugged den, where Nature's hand
Had careless strewed the rocks, a dreadful
      cave,
Whose concave ceiling echoed to the floods
Their hollow murmurs on the trembling shore,
Demanded our approach. The yawning porch
Its massy sides disclosed, and o'er the top
The ivy tendrils twined th' uncultured fern.
Fearful, we pry into the dreary vault,
Hoary with age, and breathing noxious damps.
Here screeching owls may unmolested dwell
In solitary gloom :—for few there are
Whose inclination leads them to review
A cell where putrid smells infectious reign *.

Then, turning westward, we our course pur-
      sue
Along the course of Fortha's briny flood,

* A large cave at a small distance from Kinghorn, sup-
posed, about a century ago, to have been the haunt of
thieves.

Till we o'ertake the gradual rising dale
Where fair *Burntisland* rears her reverend dome:
And here the vulgar sign-post, painted o'er
With imitations vile of man and horse ;
Of small-beer frothing o'er th' unshapely jug;
With courteous invitation, spoke us fair
To enter in, and taste what precious drops
Were there reserved to moisten strangers'
        throats,
Too often parched upon the tedious way.

After regaling here with sober cann,
Our limbs we plied, and nimbly measured o'er
The hills, the vales, and the extensive plains,
Which form the distance from *Burntisland's* port
To *Inverkeithing*. Westward still we went,
Till in the ferry-boat we lolled at ease :
Nor did we long on Neptune's empire float ;
For scarce ten posting minutes were elapsed
Till we again on *terra firma* stood,
And to M'Laren's marched, where roasted
        lamb,
With cooling lettice, crowned our social board.
Here, too, the cheering glass, chief foe to Care,
Went briskly round ; and many a virgin fair
Received our homage in a bumper full.

Thus having sacrificed a jocund hour
To smiling Mirth, we quit the happy scene,
And move progressive to Edina's walls.

Now still returning eve creeped gradual on,
And the bright sun, as weary of the sky,
Beamed forth a languid occidental ray,
Whose ruby-tinctured radiance faintly gleamed
Upon the airy cliffs and distant spires,
That float on the horizon's utmost verge.
So we, with festive joints and lingering pace,
Moved slowly on, and did not reach the town
Till Phœbus had unyoked his prancing steeds.

Ye sons of Caledonia! who delight,
With all the pomp and pageantry of state,
To roll along in gilded affluence,
For one poor moment wean your thoughts from
     these,
And list this humble strain.—If you, like us,
Could brave the angry waters; be uproused
By the first salutation to the morn
Paid by the watchful cock; or be compelled
On foot to wander o'er the lonely plain
For twenty tedious miles; then should the Gout,
With all his racking pangs, forsake your frame.
For he delights not to traverse the field,
Or rugged steep, but prides him to recline
On the luxuriance of a velvet fold,
Where Indolence on purple sofa lolls.

A BURLESQUE ELEGY,

On the Amputation of a Student's Hair before his Orders.

O SAD catastrophe! O event dire!
   How shall the loss, the heavy loss, be borne?
Or how the Muse attune the plaintive lyre,
   To sing of Strephon with his ringlets shorn?

Say ye, who can divine the mighty cause,
   From whence this modern circumcision
      springs?
Why such oppressive and such rigid laws
   Are still attendant on religious things?

Alas, poor Strephon! to the stern decree
   Which prunes your tresses, are you doomed
      to yield?
Soon shall your *caput,* like the blasted tree,
   Diffuse its faded honours o'er the field.

Now let the solemn sounds of mourning swell,
  And wake sad echoes to prolong the lay;
For, hark! methinks I hear the tragic knell;
  This hour bespeaks the barber on his way.

O razor! yet thy poignant edge suspend;
  O yet indulge me with a short delay;
Till I once more pourtray my youthful friend,
  Ere his proud locks are scattered on the
    clay;—

Ere the huge *wig*, in formal curls arrayed,
  With pulvile pregnant, shall o'ershade his
    face;
Or, like the wide umbrella, lend its aid,
  To banish lustre from the sacred place.

Mourn, O ye zephyrs! for, alas! no more
  His waving ringlets shall your call obey!
For, ah! the stubborn wig must now be wore,
  Since Strephon's locks are scattered on the
    clay.

Amanda, too, in bitter anguish sighs,
  And grieves the metamorphosis to see.
Mourn not, Amanda! for the hair that lies
  Dead on the ground, shall be revived for
    thee.

Some skilful artist of a French *frizeur*,
  With graceful ringlets shall thy temples bind,
And cull the precious relics from the floor,
  Which yet may flutter in the wanton wind.

THE

CANONGATE PLAYHOUSE in RUINS,

A BURLESQUE POEM.

Ye few, whose feeling hearts are ne'er estranged
From soft emotions ! ye who often wear
The eye of Pity, and oft vent her sighs,
When sad Melpomene, in woe-fraught strains,
Gains entrance to the breast ; or often smile
When brisk Thalia gaily trips along
Scenes of enlivening mirth ; attend my song !
And Fancy, thou whose ever-flaming light
Can penetrate into the dark abyss
Of chaos and of hell ; O ! with thy blazing
     torch

The wasteful scene illumine, that the Muse
With daring pinions may her flight pursue,
Nor with timidity be known to soar
O'er the theatric world, to chaos changed.

   Can I contemplate on those dreary scenes
Of mouldering desolation, and forbid
The voice elegiac, and the falling tear!
No more, from box to box, the basket, piled
With oranges as radiant as the spheres,
Shall with their luscious virtues charm the
     sense
Of taste and smell. No more the gaudy beau
With handkerchief in lavender well drenched,
Or *bergamot*, or *rose-watero* pure,
With flavoriferous sweets shall chase away
The pestilential fumes of vulgar cits,
Who, in impatience for the curtain's rise,
Amused the lingering moments, and applied
Thirst-quenching porter to their parched lips.

   Alas! how sadly altered is the scene!
For, lo! those sacred walls, that late were
     brushed
By rustling silks and waving capuchines,
Are now become the sport of wrinkled Time!
Those walls, that late have echoed to the voice
Of stern King Richard, to the seat transformed
Of crawling spiders and detested moths,

Who in the lonely crevices reside,
Or gender in the beams, that have upheld
Gods, demi-gods, and all the joyous crew
Of thunderers in the galleries above.

   O Shakespeare! where are all thy tinselled
      kings,
Thy fawning courtiers, and thy waggish clowns?
Where all thy fairies, spirits, witches, fiends,
That here have gambolled in nocturnal sport,
Round the lone oak, or sunk in fear away
From the shrill summons of the cock at morn?
Where now the temples, palaces, and towers?
Where now the groves that ever verdant
      smiled?
Where now the streams that never ceased to
      flow?
Where now the clouds, the rains, the hails,
      the winds,
The thunders, lightnings, and the tempests
      strong?

   Here shepherds, lolling in their woven bowers,
In dull *recitativo* often sung
Their loves, accompanied with clangour strong
From horns, from trumpets, clarinets, bas-
      soons;
From violinos sharp, or droning bass,
Or the brisk tinkling of a harpsichord.

Such is thy power, O Music! such thy fame,
That it has fabled been, how foreign song,
Soft issuing from Tenducci's slender throat,
Has drawn a plaudit from the gods enthroned
Round the empyreum of Jove himself,
High seated on Olympus' airy top.
Nay, that his feverous voice was known to
    sooth
The shrill-toned prating of the females' tongues,
Who, in obedience to the lifeless song,
All prostrate fell; all, fainting, died away
In silent ecstasies of passing joy.

Ye, who oft wander by the silver light
Of sister Luna, or to church-yard's gloom,
Or cypress shades, if Chance should guide
    your steps
To this sad mansion, think not that you tread
Unconsecrated paths; for on this ground
Have holy streams been poured, and flowerets
    strewed;
While many a kingly diadem, I ween,
Lies useless here entombed, with heaps of coin
Stamped in theatric mint;—offenceless gold!
That carried not persuasion in its hue,
To tutor mankind in their evil ways.
After a lengthened series of years,
When the unhallowed spade shall discompose
This mass of earth, then relics shall be found,

Which, or for gems of worth, or Roman coins,
Well may obtrude on antiquary's eye.
Ye spouting blades! regard this ruined fane,
And nightly come within those naked walls,
To shed the tragic tear. Full many a drop
Of precious inspiration have you sucked
From its dramatic sources. Oh! look here,
Upon this roofless and forsaken pile,
And stalk in pensive sorrow o'er the ground
Where you've beheld so many noble scenes.

Thus when the mariner to foreign clime
His bark conveys, where odoriferous gales,
And orange groves, and love-inspiring wine,
Have oft repaid his toil; if earthquake dire,
With hollow groanings and convulsive pangs,
The ground hath rent, and all those beauties
            foiled ;
Will he refrain to shed the grateful drop ;
A tribute justly due (tho' seldom paid)
To the blest memory of happier times ?

THE PEASANT, THE HEN, AND YOUNG DUCKS,

A FABLE.

A HEN, of all the dunghill crew
The fairest, stateliest to view,
Of laying tired, she fondly begs
Her keeper's leave to hatch her eggs.
He, dunned with the incessant cry,
Was forced for peace' sake to comply :—
And, in a month, the downy brood
Came chirping round the hen for food,
Who viewed them with parental eyes
Of pleasing fondness and surprise,
And was not at a loss to trace
Her likeness growing in their face ;
Tho' the broad *bills* could well declare
That they another's offspring were :
So strong will prejudices blind,
And lead astray the easy mind.

To the green margin of the brook
The hen her fancied children took :
Each young one shakes his unfledged wings,
And to the flood by instinct springs :
With willing strokes they gladly swim,
Or dive into the glassy stream,
While the fond mother vents her grief,
And prays the peasant's kind relief.
The peasant heard the bitter cries,
And thus in terms of rage replies :
" You fool! give o'er your useless moan,
" Nor mourn misfortunes not your own ;
" But learn in wisdom to forsake
" The offspring of the duck and drake."
To whom the hen, with angry crest
And scornful looks, herself addrest :
" If *reason* were my constant guide,
" (Of man the ornament and pride)
" Then should I boast a cruel heart,
" That feels not for another's smart :
" But since poor I, by *instinct* blind,
" Can boast no feelings so refined,
" 'Tis hoped your reason will excuse,
" Tho' I your counsel sage refuse,
" And from the perils of the flood
" Attempt to save another's brood."

MORAL.

When Pity, generous nymph ! possessed,
And moved at will the human breast,

No tongue its distant sufferings told,
But she assisted, she condoled,
And willing bore her tender part
In all the feelings of the heart:
But now from her our hearts decoyed,
To sense of others' woes destroyed,
-Act only from a selfish view,
Nor give the aid to pity due.

FASHION.

Bred up where discipline most rare is,
In military garden, Paris.

HUDIBRAS.

O NATURE, parent goddess! at thy shrine,
Prone to the earth, the Muse, in humble song,
Thy aid implores: nor will she wing her flight,
Till thou, bright form! in thy effulgence pure,
Deignest to look down upon her lowly state,
And shed thy powerful influence benign.

Come, then, regardless of vain Fashion's
        fools ;
Of all those vile enormities of shape
That crowd the world ; and with thee bring
Wisdom, in sober contemplation clad,
To lash those bold usurpers from the stage.

On that gay spot, where the Parisian dome
To fools the stealing hand of Time displays,
FASHION her empire holds ; a goddess great!
View her, amidst the *Millinerian* train,
On a resplendent throne exalted high,
Strangely diversified with gewgaw forms.
Her busy hand glides pleasurably o'er
The darling novelties, the trinkets rare,
That greet the sight of the admiring dames,
Whose dear-bought treasures o'er their native isle
Contagious spread, infect the wholesome air
That cherished vigour in Britannia's sons.

Near this proud seat of Fashion's antic form
A sphere revolves, on whose bright orb behold
The circulating mode of changeful dress,
Which, like the image of the Sun himself,
Glories in coursing thro' the diverse signs
Which blazon in the zodiac of heaven.
Around her throne coquets and petit beaux
Unnumbered shine, and with each other vie
In nameless ornaments and gaudy plumes.

O worthy emulation! to excel
In trifles such as these : how truly great!
Unworthy of the peevish blubbering boy,
Crushed in his childhood by the fondling nurse,
Who, for some favourite bawble, frets and
    pines.

  Amongst the proud attendants of this shrine,
The wealthy, young, and gay Clarinda, draws
From poorer objects the astonished eye.
Her looks, her dress, and her affected mein,
Speak her enthusiast keen in Fashion's train.
White as the covered Alps, or wintry face
Of snowy Lapland, her toupée upreared,
Exhibits to the view a cumbrous mass
Of curls high nodding o'er her polished brow;
From which redundant flows the Brussels' lace,
With pendant ribbons, too, of various dye,
Where all the colours in th' ethereal bow
Unite, and blend, and tantalize the sight.

  Nature! to thee alone, not Fashion's pomp,
Does Beauty owe her all-commanding eye.
From the green bosom of the watery main,
Arrayed by thee, majestic Venus rose,
With waving ringlets carelessly diffused,
Floating luxuriant o'er the restless surge.
What Rubens then, with his enlivening hand,
Could paint the bright vermilion of her cheek,

Pure as the roseate portal of the east,
That opens to receive the cheering ray
Of Phœbus beaming from the orient sky!
For sterling Beauty needs no faint essays,
Or colourings of art, to gild her more:—
She is all-perfect.—And if Beauty fail,
Where are those ornaments, those rich attires,
Which can reflect a lustré on that face,
Where she with light innate disdains to shine?

Britons! beware of Fashion's luring wiles:
On either hand, chief guardians of her power,
And sole dictators of her fickle voice,
Folly and dull Effeminacy reign;
Whose blackest magic and unhallowed spells
The Roman ardour checked; their strength
        decayed,
And all their glory scattered to the winds.

Tremble, O Albion! for the voice of Fate
Seems ready to decree thy after fall.
By pride, by luxury, what fatal ills,
Unheeded, have approached thy mortal frame!
How many foreign weeds their heads have
        reared
In thy fair garden! Hasten, ere their strength
And baneful vegetation taint the soil,
To root out rank disease, which soon must
        spread,

If no blessed antidote will purge away
Fashion's proud minions from our sea-girt isle.

====

ON THE DEATH OF

MR THOMAS LANCASHIRE,

Comedian.

ALAS, poor Tom! how oft, with merry heart,
Have we beheld thee play the Sexton's part?
Each comic heart must now be grieved to see
The Sexton's dreary part performed on thee.

====

ON SEEING A LADY PAINT HERSELF.

WHEN, by some misadventure crossed,
The banker hath his fortune lost,
Credit his instant need supplies,
And for a moment blinds our eyes:

So Delia, when her beauty's flown,
Trades on a bottom not her own,
And labours to escape detection,
By putting on a false complexion.

———

EXTEMPORE,

On seeing Stanzas addressed to MRS HARTLEY,
Comedian, wherein she is described as resembling
MARY QUEEN OF SCOTS.

HARTLEY resembles Scotland's Queen,
  Some bard enraptured cries ;
A flattering bard he is, I ween,
  Or else the Painter lies.

A TAVERN ELEGY.

Fled are the moments of delusive Mirth;
   The fancied pleasure! paradise divine!
Hushed are the clamours that derive their birth
   From generous floods of soul-reviving wine.

Still night and silence now succeed their noise;
   The erring tides of passion rage no more;
But all is peaceful as the ocean's voice
   When breezeless waters kiss the silent shore.

Here stood the juice, whose care-controlling
      powers
   Could every human misery subdue,
And wake to sportive joy the lazy hours,
   That to the languid senses hateful grew.

Attracted by the magic of the bowl,
   Around the swelling brim in full array
The glasses circled, as the planets roll
   And hail with borrowed light the god of day.

Here Music, the delight of moments gay,
  Bade the unguarded tongues their motions
      cease,
And with a mirthful, a melodious lay,
  Awed the fell voice of Discord into peace.

These are the joys that Virtue must approve,
  While Reason shines with majesty divine,
Ere our ideas in disorder move,
  And sad excess against the soul combine.

What evils have not frantic mortals done
  By wine, that *ignis fatuus* of the mind!
How many by its force to Vice are won,
  Since first ordained to tantalize mankind!

By Bacchus' power, ye sons of Riot! say,
  How many watchful sentinels have bled?
How many travellers have lost their way,
  By lamps unguided thro' the evening shade?

O spare those friendly twinklers of the night!
  Let no rude cane their hallowed orbs assail!
For Cowardice alone condemns the light,
  That shows her countenance aghast and
      pale.

Now the short taper warns me to depart
  Ere Darkness shall assume his dreary sway;

Ere Solitude fall heavy on my heart,
   That lingers for the far approach of day.

Who would not welcome the less dreaded doom,
   To be for ever numbered with the dead,
Rather than bear the miserable gloom,
   When all his comforts, all his friends, are fled.

Bear me, ye gods! where I may calmly rest
   From all the follies of the night secure,
The balmy blessings of repose to taste,
   Nor hear the tongue of Outrage at my door.

GOOD EATING.

HEAR, O ye host of Epicurus! hear!
Each portly form, whose overhanging paunch
Can well denote the all-transcendant joy
That springs unbounded from fruition full
Of rich repast;—to you I consecrate
The song adventurous;—happy if the Muse
Can cook the numbers to your palates keen,
Or send but half the relish with her song,
That smoking sirloins to your souls convey.

Hence now, ye starvelings wan! whose empty
    sides
Oft echo to the hollow-murmuring tones
Of hunger fell.—Avaunt, ye base-born hinds!
Whose fates unkind ne'er destined you to gorge
The banquet rare, or wage a pleasing war
With the delicious morsels of the earth.
To you I sing not :—for, alas! what pain,
What tantalizing tortures would ensue,
To aid the force of Famine's sharpest tooth,
Were I to breathe my accents in your ear!

Hail, Roast Beef! monarch of the festive
    throng,
To Hunger's bane the strongest antidote ;
Come, and with all thy rage-appeasing sweets
Our appetites allay! For, or attended
By root Hibernian, or plum-pudding rare,
Still thou art welcome to the social board.
Say, can the spicy gales from Orient blown,
Or Zephyr's wing, that from the orange groves
Brushes the breeze, with rich perfumes replete,
More aromatic or reviving smell
To nostrils bring? Or can the glassy streams
Of Pactolus, that o'er his golden sands
Delightful glide, thy luscious drops out-vie,
That from thy sides imbrowned unnumbered
    fall ?
Behold, at thy approach, what smiles serene

Beam from the ravish'd guests !—Still are their
      tongues,
While they, with whetted instruments, prepare
For deep incision.—Now the abscess bleeds,
And the devouring band, with stomachs keen,
And glutting rage, thy beauteous form destroy;
Leave you a skeleton, marrowless and bare,
A prey to dunghills, or vexatious sport
Of torrent rushing from Defilement's urns,
That o'er the city's flinty pavement hurls.

So fares it with the man, whose powerful pelf
Once could command respect. Caressed by all,
His bounties were as lavish as the hand
Of yellow Ceres, till his stores decayed :
And, then, (O dismal tale!) those precious drops
Of flattery, that bedew'd his spring of fortune,
Leave the sad winter of his state so fallen,
Nor nurse the thorn from which they ne'er can
      hope
Again to pluck the odour-dropping rose!

For thee, Roast Beef! in variegated shapes,
Have mortals toiled.—The sailor sternly braves
The strength of Boreas, and exulting stands
Upon the sea-washed deck. With hopes inspired
Of yet indulging in thy wished-for sweets,
He smiles amidst the dangers that surround him ;

Cheerful he steers to cold forbidden climes;
Or to the torrid zone explores his way.

    Be kind, ye Powers! and still, propitious,
       send
This paragon of feeding to our halls.
With this regaled, who would, vain-glorious,
       wish
For towering pyramids superbly crowned
With jellies, syllabubs, or ice-creams rare?
These can amuse the eye, and may bestow
A short-lived pleasure to a palate strange:
But, for a moment's pleasure, who would vend
A lifetime that would else be spent in joy,
For hateful loathings, and for gouty rheums,
Ever preceded by indulged excess?

    Blest be those walls, where Hospitality
And Welcome reign at large! There may you oft
Of social cheer partake, and love, and joy;
Pleasures that to the human mind convey
Ideal pictures of the bliss supreme:
But near the gate where Parsimony dwells,
Where Ceremony cool, with brow austere,
Confronts the guests, ne'er let thy foot approach!
Deprived of thee, heaven-born Benevolence!
What is life's garden but a devious wild,
Thro' which the traveller must pass forlorn,
Unguided by the aid of Friendship's ray?

Rather, if Poverty hold converse with thee,
To the lone garret's lofty bield ascend,
Or dive to some sad cell:—there have recourse
To meagre offals, where, tho' small thy fare,
Freedom shall wing thee to a purer joy
Than banquets with superfluous dainties
        crowned,
Mixed with reserve and coolness, can afford.

But, if your better fortunes have prepared
Your purse with ducats, and with health your
        frame,
Assemble friends! and to the tavern straight,
Where the officious drawer, bending low,
Is passive to a fault. Then, nor the Signior
        Grand,
Nor Russia's Empress, signalized for war,
Can govern with more arbitrary sway.
Ye, who for health, for exercise, for air,
Oft saunter from Edina's smoke-capt spires,
And by the grassy hill, or dimpled brook,
An appetite revive, should often stray
O'er Arthur's-seat's green pastures, to the town
For sheepheads and bone-bridges famed of yore,
That in our country's annals stands yclept,
Fair Duddingstonia, where you may be blessed
With simple fare and vegetable sweets,
Freed from the clamours of the busy world.

Or, if for recreation you should stray
To Leithian shore, and breathe the keener air
Wafted from Neptune's empire of the main ;
If appetite invite, and cash prevail,
Ply not your joints upon the homeward tract,
Till Lawson, chiefest of the Scottish hosts !
To nimblefooted waiters give command
The cloth to lay.— Instinctively they come ;
And lo ! the table, wrapt in cloudy steams,
Groans with the weight of the transporting fare,
That breathes frankincense on the guests around.

Now, while stern Winter holds his frigid sway,
And to a period spins the closing year ;
While festivals abound, and sportive hours
Kill the remembrance of our waning time,
Let not Intemperance, destructive fiend !
Gain entrance to our halls. Despoiled by him,
Shall cloyed appetite, forerunner sad
Of rank disease, inveterate clasp your frame.
Contentment shall no more be known to spread
Her cherub wings round thy once happy dwell-
    ing,
But misery of thought, and racking pain,
Shall plunge you headlong to the dark abyss.

TEA.

Ye maidens modest! on whose sullen brows
Hath weaning Chastity her wrinkles cull'd;
Who constant labour o'er consumptive oil,
At midnight knell, to wash Sleep's nightly balm
From closing eyelids, with the grateful drops
Of Tea's blessed juices; list th' obsequious lays,
That come not, with Parnassian honors crowned,
To dwell in murmurs o'er your sleepy sense;
But, fresh from Orient blown, to chase far off
Your lethargy; that dormant needles, rous'd,
May pierce the waving mantua's silken folds.
For many a dame, in chamber sadly pent,
Hath this reviving liquor called to life:
And well it did, to mitigate the frowns
Of anger, reddening on Lucinda's brow
With flash malignant, that had harbour'd there,
If she at masquerade, or play, or ball,
Appeared not in her newest, best attire.
But Venus, goddess of th' eternal smile,

Knowing that stormy brows but ill become
Fair patterns of her beauty, hath ordained
Celestial Tea;—a fountain that can cure
The ills of passion, and can free from frowns,
And sobs, and sighs, the disappointed fair.

To her, ye fair! in adoration bow!
Whether at blushing morn, or dewy eve,
Her smoking cordials greet your fragrant board,
With Hyson, or Bohea, or Congo, crowned.
At midnight skies, ye mantua-makers! hail
The sacred offering.—For the haughty belles
No longer can upbraid your lingering hands,
With trains upborne aloft by dusty gales
That sweep the ball-room. Swift they glide
    along,
And, with their sailing streamers, catch the eye
Of some Adonis, marked to love a prey.
Whose bosom ne'er had panted with a sigh,
But for the silken draperies that enclose
Graces from Fancy's eye but ill concealed.

Mark well the fair! observe their modest eye,
With all the innocence of beauty blessed.
Could Slander o'er that tongue its power retain,
Whose breath is Music?—Ah, fallacious
    thought!
The surface is Ambrosia's mingled sweets;
But all below is death. At tea-board met,

Attend their prattling tongues;—they scoff,—
    they rail
Unbounded; but their darts are chiefly aimed
At some gay fair, whose beauties far eclipse
Her dim beholders; who, with haggard eyes,
Would blight those charms where raptures long
    have dwelt
In ecstacy, delighted and sufficed.

In vain hath Beauty, with her varied robe,
Bestowed her glowing blushes o'er her cheeks,
And called attendant Graces to her aid,
To blend the scarlet and the lily fair.
In vain did Venus in her favourite mould
Adapt the slender form to Cupid's choice.—
When Slander comes, her blasts too fatal prove;
Pale are those cheeks where youth and beauty
    glowed;
Where smiles, where freshness, and where roses
    grew:
Ghastly and wan their Gorgon picture comes,
With every fury grinning from the looks
Of frightful monster. Envy's hissing tongue
With deepest vengeance wounds, and every
    wound
With deeper canker, deeper poison, teems.

O Gold! thy luring lustre first prevailed
On man to tempt the fretful winds and waves,

And hunt new fancies. Still, thy glaring form
Bids Commerce thrive, and o'er the Indian
    waves,
O'er-stemming danger, draw the laboring keel,
From China's coast to Britain's colder clime,
Fraught with the fruits and herbage of her vales.
In them whatever vegetable springs,
How loathsome and corrupted, triumphs here,
The bane of life, of health the sure decay :
Yet, yet we swallow, and extol the draught,
Tho' nervous ails should spring, and vaporish
    qualms
Our senses and our appetites destroy.

Look round, ye sipplers of the poisoned cup
From foreign plant distilled ! No more repine
That Nature, sparing of her sacred sweets,
Hath doomed you in a wilderness to dwell ;
While round Britannia's streams she kindly
    rears
Green sage, and wild thyme.—These were
    sure decreed,
As plants of Britain, to regale her sons
With native moisture, more refreshing sweet,
And more profuse of health and vigor's balm,
Than all the stems that India can boast.

THE SOW OF FEELING.

Well! I protest there's no such thing as dealing
With these starched poets,—with these Men of Feeling!
EPILOGUE TO THE PRINCE OF TUNIS.

MALIGNANT planets! do ye still combine
Against this wayward, dreary life of mine?
Has pitiless Oppression—cruel case!
Gained sole possession of the human race?
By cruel hands has every virtue bled,
And Innocence from men to vultures fled!

Thrice happy, had I lived in Jewish time,
When swallowing pork or pig was deemed a
        crime;
My husband long had blessed my longing arms,
Long, long had known love's sympathetic
        charms!
My children, too,—a little suckling race,
With all their father growing in their face,

From their prolific dam had ne'er been torn,
Nor to the bloody stalls of butchers borne.

Ah, Luxury ! to you my being owes
Its load of misery,—its load of woes !
With heavy heart I saunter all the day ;
Gruntle and murmur all my hours away !
In vain I try to summon old desire
For favourite sports,—for wallowing in the mire:
Thoughts of my husband, of my children slain,
Turn all my wonted pleasure into pain !
How oft did we, in Phœbus' warming ray,
Bask on the humid softness of the clay ?
Oft did his lusty head defend my tail
From the rude whispers of the angry gale ;
While nose-refreshing puddles streamed around,
And floating odours hailed the dung-clad
            ground.

Near by a rustic mill's enchanting clack,
Where plenteous bushels load the peasant's back,
In straw-crowned hovel, there to life we came,
One boar our father, and one sow our dam.
While tender infants on our mother's breast,
A flame divine in either shone confest :
In riper hours love's more than ardent blaze,
Inkindled all his passion, all his praise !
No deadly, sinful passion fired his soul ;
Virtue o'er all his actions gained control !

That cherub which attracts the female heart,
And makes them soonest with their beauty part,
Attracted mine ;—I gave him all my love,
In the recesses of a verdant grove ;
'Twas there I listened to his warmest vows,
Amidst the pendant melancholy boughs ;
'Twas there my trusty lover shook for me
A shower of acorns from the oaken tree ;
And from the teeming earth, with joy, ploughed
      out,
The roots salabrious with his hardy snout.

But Happiness ! a floating meteor, thou,
That still inconstant art to man and sow,
Left us in gloomiest horrors to reside,
Near by the deep-dyed sanguinary tide,
Where whetting steel prepares the butchering
      knives,
With greater ease to take the harmless lives
Of cows, and calves, and sheep, and hogs, who
      fear
The bite of bull-dogs, that incessant tear
Their flesh, and keenly suck the blood-distil-
      ling ear !

At length, the day, the eventful day, drew
      near,
Detested cause of many a briny tear !

I'll weep, till sorrow shall my eye-lids drain,
A tender husband and a brother slain !
Alas, the lovely languor of his eye,
When the base murderers bore him captive by!
His mournful voice, the music of his groans,
Had melted any hearts—but hearts of stones !
Oh ! had some angel at that instant come,
Given me four nimble fingers and a thumb,
The blood-stained blade I'd turned upon his foe,
And sudden sent him to the shades below,—
Where, or Pythagoras' opinion jests,
Beasts are made butchers,—butchers changed
    to beasts.

Wisely in early times the law decreed,
For human food few quadrupeds should bleed !
But monstrous man, still erring from the laws,
The curse of heaven upon his banquet draws!
Already has he drained the marshes dry,
For frogs, new victims of his luxury ;
And soon the toad and lizard may come home,
In his voracious paunch to find a tomb.
Cats, rats, and mice, their destiny may mourn ;
In time their carcases on spits may turn ;
They may rejoice to-day,—While I resign
Life, to be numbered 'mongst the FEELING
    SWINE.

THE BUGS.

Thou source of song sublime! thou chiefest
    Muse!
Whose sacred fountain of immortal fame
Bedewed the flowerets culled for Homer's brow,
When he on Grecian plains the battles sung
Of frogs and mice : Do thou, thro' Fancy's
    maze
Of sportive pastime, lead a lowly Muse
Her rites to join, while, with a faultering voice,
She sings of reptiles yet in song unknown.

    Nor you, ye bards! who oft have struck the
    lyre,
And tuned it to the movement of the spheres
In harmony divine, reproach the lays ;
Which, tho' they wind not thro' the starry
    host
Of bright creation, or on earth delight
To haunt the murmuring cadence of the floods

Thro' scenes where Nature, with a hand pro-
fuse,
Hath lavish strewed her gems of precious dye;
Yet, in the small existence of a gnat,
Or tiny bug, doth she, with equal skill,
If not transcending, stamp her wonders there,
Only disclosed to microscopic eye.

Of old the Dryads near Edina's walls
Their mansions reared, and groves unnumbered
rose
Of branching oak, spread beach, and lofty
pine;
Under whose shade, to shun the noontide blaze,
Did Pan resort, with all his rural train
Of shepherds and of nymphs.—The Dryads
pleased,
Would hail their sports, and summon Echo's
voice
To send her greetings thro' the waving woods;
But the rude ax, long brandished by the hand
Of daring innovation, shaved the lawns;
Then not a thicket or a copse remained
To sigh in concert with the breeze of eve.

Edina's mansions, with lignarian art,
Were piled and fronted.—Like an ark she
seemed
To lie on mountain's top, with shapes replete,

Clean and unclean, that daily wander o'er
Her streets, that once were spacious, once were
     gay.
To Jove the Dryads prayed, nor prayed in
     vain,
For vengeance on her sons —At midnight drear
Black showers descend, and teeming myriads
     rise
Of bugs abhorrent, who by instinct steal
Thro' the putrescent and corrosive pores
Of sapless trees, that late in forest stood,
With all the majesty of summer crowned.

  By Jove's command dispersed, they wander
     wide
O'er all the city.—Some their cells prepare
'Mid the rich trappings and the gay attire
Of state luxuriant, and are fond to press
The waving canopy's depending folds ;
While others, destined to an humbler fate,
Seek shelter from the dwellings of the poor,
Plying their nightly suction to the bed
Of toiled mechanic, who, with folded arms,
Enjoys the comforts of a sleep so sound,
That not the alarming sting of glutting bug
To murderous deed can rouse his brawny arm
Upon the blood-swoln fiend, who basely steals
Life's genial current from his throbbing veins.

Happy were Grandeur, could she triumph
    here,
And banish from her halls each misery,
Which she must brook in common with the
    poor,
Who beg subsistence from her sparing hands.
Then might the rich, to fell disease unknown,
Indulge in fond excess, nor ever feel
The slowly-creeping hours of restless night,
When shook with guilty horrors.—But the
    wind,
Whose fretful gusts of anger shake the world,
Bears more destructive on the aspiring roofs
Of dome and palace, than on cottage low,
That meets Æolus with his gentler breath,
When safely sheltered in the peaceful vale.

Is there a being breathes, howe'er so vile,
Too pitiful for Envy?—She, with venomed
    tooth,
And grinning madness, frowns upon the bliss
Of every species;—from the human form
That spurns the earth, and bends his mental
    eye
Thro' the profundity of space unknown,
Down to the crawling bug's detested race.

Thus the lover pines, that reptile rude
Should, 'mid the lilies of fair Chloe's breast,

Implant the deep carnation, and enjoy
Those sweets which angel modesty hath veiled
From eyes profane.—Yet murmur not, ye few
Who gladly would be bugs for Chloe's sake!
For soon, alas! the fluctuating gales
Of earthly joy invert the happy scene.
The breath of Spring may, with her balmy
     power,
And warmth diffusive, give to Nature's face
Her brightest colours ;—but how short the
     space,
Till angry Eurus, from his petrid cave,
Deform the year, and all these sweets annoy!

    Even so befals it to this creeping race;
This envied commonwealth.—For they a while
On Chloe's bosom, alabaster fair,
May steal ambrosial bliss; or may regale
On the rich viands of luxurious blood,
Delighted and sufficed. But mark the end:
Lo! Whitsuntide appears, with gloomy train
Of growing desolation.—First, Upholsterer rude
Removes the waving drapery, where, for years,
A thriving colony of old and young
Had hid their numbers from the prying day.
Anon they fall, and gladly would retire
To safer ambush; but his ruthless foot,
Ah, cruel pressure! cracks their vital springs,
And with their deep-dyed scarlet smears the
     floor.

Sweet Powers! has Pity in the female breast
No tender residence,—no loved abode,—
To urge from murderous deed the avenging
 hand
Of angry house-maid?—She'll have blood for
 blood!
For, lo! the boiling streams from copper tube,
Hot as her rage, sweep myriads to death.
Their carcases are destined to the urn
Of some chaste Naiad, that gives birth to
 floods,
Whose fragrant virtues hail Edina, famed
For yenow limpid,—whose chaste name the
 Muse
Deems too exalted to retail in song.

 Ah me! no longer they, at midnight shade,
With baneful sting, shall seek the downy couch
Of slumbering mortals.—Nor shall love-sick
 swain,
When, by the bubbling brook, in fairy dream,
His nymph, but half reluctant to his wish,
Is gently folded in his eager arms,
E'er curse the shaft envenomed, that disturbs
His long-loved fancies.—Nor shall hungry bard,
Whose strong imagination, whetted keen,
Conveys him to the feast, be tantalized
With poisonous tortures, when the cup, brim-
 ful

Of purple vintage, gives him greater joy
Than all the Heliconian streams that play
And murmur round Parnassus. Now the
    wretch,
Oft doomed to restless days and sleepless nights,
By bugbear Conscience thralled, enjoys an hour
Of undisturbed repose.—The Miser, too,
May brook his golden dreams, nor wake with
    fear
That thieves or kindred (for no soul he'll trust)
Have broke upon his chest, and strive to steal
The shining idols of his useless hours.

Happy the bug, whose unambitious views
To gilded pomp ne'er tempt him to aspire!
Safely may he, enwrapt in russet fold
Of cobwebbed curtain, set at bay the fears
That still attendant are on bugs of state.
He never knows at morn the busy brush
Of scrubbing chambermaid. His coursing
    blood
Is ne'er obstructed with obnoxious dose,
By Oliphant prepared,—too poisonous drug!
As fatal to this hated crawling tribe
As ball and powder to the sons of war.

AN EXPEDITION TO

FIFE AND THE ISLAND OF MAY,

On board the BLESSED ENDEAVOUR *of Dunbar,*
Captain ROXBURGH *Commander.*

LIST, O ye slumberers on the peaceful shore!
Whose lives are one unvariegated calm
Of stillness and of sloth : and hear, O nymph!
In heaven ycleped Pleasure : from your throne
Effulgent send a heavenly radiant beam,
That, cheered by thee, the Muse may bend
   her way :
For from no earthly flight she builds her song,
But from the bosom of green Neptune's main
Would fain emerge, and under Phœbe's reign,
Transmit her numbers to inclining ears.

 Now, when the warbling songsters quit the
   groves,
And solemn-sounding whisperings lull the spray,

To meditation sacred, let me roam
O'er the blessed floods that wash our natal
    shore,
And view the wonders of the deep profound,
While now the western breezes reign around,
And Boreas, sleeping in his iron cave,
Regains his strength and animated rage,
To wake new tempests, and inswell new seas.

And now Favonius wings the sprightly gale;
The willing canvas, swelling with the breeze,
Gives life and motion to our bounding prow,
While the hoarse boatswain's pipe, shrill-sound-
    ing far,
Calls all the tars to action.   Hardy sons!
Who shudder not at life's devouring gales,
But smile amidst the tempest's sounding jars,
Or 'midst the hollow thunders of the war.
Fresh sprung from Greenland's cold, they hail
    with joy
The happier clime, the fresh autumnal breeze,
By Syrius guided, to allay the heat,
That else would parch the vigour of their veins.
Hard change, alas! from petrifying cold
Instant to plunge to the severest ray
That burning Dog-star, or bright Phœbus sheds.
Like comet whirling thro' the ethereal void,
Now they are reddened with the solar blaze,
Now froze and tortured by the frigid zone.

Thrice happy Britons! whose well-tempered
    clay
Can face all climes, all tempests, and all seas.
These are the sons that check the growing war;
These are the sons that hem Britannia round
From sudden innovation ;—awe the shores,
And make their drooping pendants hail her
    queen
And mistress of the globe.—They guard our
    beds,
While fearless we enjoy secure repose,
And all the blessings of a bounteous sky.
To them in feverous adoration bend,
Ye fashioned macaronies! whose bright blades
Were never dimmed or stained with hostile
    blood,
But still hang dangling on your feeble thigh,
While thro' the Mall or Park you shew away,
Or thro' the drawing-room on tiptoe steal.

On poop aloft, to messmates laid along,
Some son of Neptune, whose old wrinkled
    brow
Has braved the rattling thunder, tells his tale
Of dangers, sieges, and of battles dire,
While they, as Fortune favours, greet with
    smiles,
Or heave the bitter sympathetic sigh,
As the capricious fickle goddess frowns.

Ah! how unstable are the joys of life!
The pleasures, ah, how few!—Now smile the
    skies
With aspect mild; and now the thunders shake,
And all the radiance of the heavens deflower.
Thro' the small opening of the mainsail broad,
Lo, Boreas steals, and tears him from the yard,
Where long and lasting he has played his part!
So suffers Virtue. When in her fair form
The smallest flaw is found, the whole decays.
In vain she may implore with piteous eye,
And spread her naked pinions to the blast:
A reputation maimed finds no repair,
Till Death, the ghastly monarch, shuts the
    scene.

And now we gain the *May,* whose midnight
    light,
Like vestal virgins' offerings undecayed,
To mariners bewildered acts the part
Of social friendship, guiding those that err
With kindly radiance to their destined port.

Thanks, kindest Nature! for those floating
    gems,
Those green-grown isles, with which you, la-
    vish, strew
Great Neptune's empire. But for thee! the
    main

Were an uncomfortable mazy flood.
No guidance, then, would bless the steersman's
     skill,
No resting-place would crown the mariner's
     wish,
When he to distant gales his canvas spreads,
To search new wonders.—Here the verdant
     shores
Teem with new freshness, and regale our sight
With caves, that ancient time, in days of yore,
Sequestered for the haunt of Druid lone,
There to remain in solitary cell,
Beyond the power of mortals to disjoin
From holy meditation.—Happy now
To cast our eyes around from shore to shore,
While by the oozy caverns on the beach
We wander wild, and listen to the roar
Of billows murmuring with incessant noise.

And now, by Fancy led, we wander wild
Where o'er the rugged steep the buried dead
Remote lie anchored in their parent mould ;
Where a few fading willows point the state
Of man's decay.   Ah, Death ! where'er we
     fly,
Whether we seek the busy and the gay,
The mourner or the joyful, there art thou !
No distant isle, no surly swelling surge,
E'er awed thy progress, or controlled thy sway,

To bless us with that comfort, length of days,
By all aspired at, but by few attained.

To Fife we steer ; of all beneath the sun
The most unhallowed 'mid the Scotian plains!
And here (sad emblem of deceitful times!)
Hath sad Hypocrisy her standard borne.
Mirth knows no residence ; but ghastly Fear
Stands trembling and appalled at airy sights.
Once, only once ! Reward it, gracious Powers!
Did Hospitality, with open face,
And winning smile, cheer the deserted sight,
That else had languished for the blessed return
Of beauteous day, to dissipate the clouds
Of endless night, and superstition wild,
That constant hover o'er the dark abode.
O happy Lothian ! happy thrice thy sons !
Who ne'er yet ventured from the Southern
        shore
To tempt Misfortune on the Fifan coast :
Again with thee we dwell, and taste thy joys,
Where sorrow reigns not, and where every
        gale
Is fraught with fulness, blessed with living
        hope,
That fears no canker from the year's decay.

TO SIR JOHN FIELDING,

On his Attempt to suppress the Beggar's Opera.

> When you censure the age,
>   Be cautious and sage,
> Lest the courtiers offended should be ;
>   When you mention vice or bribe,
>   'Tis so pat to all the tribe,
> Each cries,—It was levelled at me.
>   GAY.

> 'Tis woman that seduces all mankind.
>   FILCH.

BENEATH what cheerful region of the sky
Shall Wit, shall Humour, and the Muses fly ?
For ours, a cold, inhospitable clime,
Refuses quarter to the Muse and rhyme.

If on her brows an envied laurel springs,
They shake its foliage ; crop her growing wings,
That with the plumes of virtue wisely soar,
And all the follies of the age explore :
But should old *Grub* her rankest venom pour,
And every virtue with a vice deflower,
Her verse is sacred, Justices agree ;
Even *Justice Fielding* signs the wise decree.

Let fortune-dealers, wise predictors ! tell
From what bright planet Justice Fielding fell,
Augusta trembles at the awful name ;
The darling tongue of Liberty is tame,
Basely confined by him in Newgate chains,
Nor dare exclaim how harshly Fielding reigns.

In days when every mercer has his scale,
To tell what pieces lack, how few prevail !
I wonder not the low-born menial trade,
By partial Justice has aside been laid ;
For she no discount gives for Virtue worn ;
Her aged joints are without mercy torn.

In vain, O Gay ! thy Muse explored the
          way
Of yore, to banish the Italian lay ;
Gave homely numbers sweet, tho' warmly
          strong ;
The British chorus blessed the happy song :

Thy manly voice, and Albion's, then, were
　　heard ;
Felt by her sons, and by her sons revered :
Eunuchs, not men, now bear aloft the palm,
And o'er our senses pour lethargic balm.

The Stage the truest mirror is of life :
Our passions there revolve in active strife ;
Each character is there displayed to view ;
Each hates his own, tho' well assured 'tis true.
No marvel, then, that all the world should
　　own
In Peachum's treachery Justice Fielding known;
Since thieves so common are, and Justice !
　　you
Thieves to the gallows for reward pursue.
Had Gay, by writing, roused the stealing
　　trade,
You'd been less active to suppress your bread :
For, trust me ! when a robber loses ground,
You lose your living with your forty pound.

'Twas woman first that snatched the luring
　　bait :
The tempter taught her to transgress and eat.
Tho' wrong the deed, her quick compunction
　　told ;
She banished Adam from an age of gold.

When women now transgress fair Virtue's
      rules,
Men are their pupils, and the stews their
      schools.
From simple whoredom greater sins began
To shoot, to bloom, to centre all in man:
Footpads on Hounslow flourish here to-day;
The next, old Tyburn sweeps them all away.
For woman's faults, the cause of every wrong,
Men robbed and murdered, thieves at Tyburn
      strung.
In panting breasts to raise the fond alarm;
Make females in the cause of virtue warm;
Gay has compared them to the Summer flower,
The boast and glory of an idle hour:
When cropped, it falls, shrinks, withers, and
      decays,
And to oblivion dark consigns its days.

Hath this a power to win the female heart
Back from its vice, from virtue ne'er to part?
If so, the wayward virgin 'twill restore;
And murders, robberies, rapes, will be no more.

These were the lays of him who Virtue
      knew;
Her dictates who revered, and practised too;
No idle theorist in her guiltless ways,
He gave the spotless goddess all his days.

O Queensberry! his best and earliest friend;
All that his wit or learning could commend;
Thou best of patrons! of his Muse the pride!
Still in her pageant shalt thou first preside;—
No idle pomp that riches can procure,
Sprung in a moment, faded in an hour,
But pageant, lasting as the uncropped bay,
That verdant triumphs with the Muse of Gay.

CHARACTER OF A FRIEND,

In an Epitaph which he desired the Author to write.

UNDER this turf, to mouldering earth con-
    signed,
Lies he, who once was fickle as the wind.
Alike the scenes of good and ill he knew,
From the chaste temple to the lewdest stew.
Virtue and Vice in him alternate reigned;—
That filled his mind, and *this* his pocket drained;
Till in the contest they so stubborn grew,
Death gave the parting blow, and both with-
    drew.

TO DR SAMUEL JOHNSON.

Food for a New Edition of his Dictionary.

Let Wilkes and Churchill rage no more,
  Tho' scarce provision, learning's good ;
What can these hungries next explore?
  Even Samuel Johnson loves our food.

GREAT Pedagogue! whose literarian lore,
With syllable on syllable conjoined,
To transmutate and varify, hast learned
The whole revolving scientific names
That in the alphabetic columns lie,
Far from the knowledge of mortalic shapes ;
As we, who never can peroculate
The miracles by thee miraculized,

The Muse, silential long, with mouth apert,
Would give vibration to stagnatic tongue,
And loud encomiate thy puissant name,
Eulogiated from the green decline
Of Thames's banks to Scoticanian shores,
Where Lochlomondian liquids undulize.

To meminate thy name in after times,
The mighty Mayor of each regalian town
Shall consignate thy work to parchment fair,
In roll burgharian, and their tables all
Shall fumigate with fumigation strong :
Scotland, from perpendicularian hills,
Shall emigrate her fair muttonian store,
Which late had there in pedestration walked,
And o'er her airy heights perambulized.

Oh, blackest execrations on thy head,
Edina shameless ! Tho' he came within
The bounds of your notation ; tho' you knew
His honorific name ; you noted not,
But basely suffered him to chariotize
Far from your towers, with smoke that nubi-
     late,
Nor drank one amicitial swelling cup
To welcome him convivial.   Bailies all !
With rage inflated, catenations * tear,

* Catenations, vide *Chains*.   JOHNSON.

Nor ever after be you vinculized,
Since you that sociability denied
To him whose potent Lexiphanian style
Words can prolongate, and inswell his page
With what in others to a line's confined.

Welcome, thou verbal potentate and prince!
To hills and valleys, where emerging oats
From earth assuage our pauperty to bay,
And bless thy name, thy dictionarian skill,
Which there definitive will still remain,
And oft be speculized by taper blue,
While youth studentious turn thy folio page.

Have you, as yet, in per'patetic mood,
Regarded with the texture of the eye
The cave cavernic, where fraternal bard,
Churchill, depicted pauperated swains
With thraldom and bleak want reducted sore ;
Where Nature, colourized, so coarsely fades,
And puts her russet par'pharnalia on ?
Have you, as yet, the way explorified,
To let lignarian chalice, swelled with oats,
Thy orifice approach ? Have you, as yet,
With skin fresh rubified with scarlet spheres,
Applied brimstonic unction to your hide,
To terrify the salamandrian fire,
That from involuntary digits asks
The strong allaceration ?—Or can you swill

The usquebalian flames of whisky blue,
In fermentation strong? Have you applied
The kilt aërian to your Anglian thighs,
And with renunciation assignized
Your breeches in Londona to be worn?
Can you, in frigour of Highlandian sky,
On heathy summi s take nocturnal rest?
It cannot be :—You may as well desire
An alderman leave plumpuddenian store,
And scratch the tegument from pottage dish,
As bid thy countrymen, and thee, conjoined,
Forsake stomachic joys.   Then hie you home,
And be a malcontent, that naked hinds,
On lentiles fed, could make your kingdom
    quake,
And tremulate Old England libertized !

EPIGRAM,

On seeing Scales used in a Mason Lodge.

Why should the Brethren, met in Lodge,
    Adopt such awkward measures,
To set their scales and weights to judge
    The value of their treasures?

The law laid down from age to age,
    How can they well o'ercome it ?
For it forbids them to engage
    With aught but Line and Plummet.

EPITAPH ON GENERAL WOLFE.

In worth exceeding, and in virtue great,
Words would want force his actions to relate.
Silence, ye bards! eulogiums vain forbear;
It is enough to say that *Wolfe lies here*.

EPIGRAM,

On the numerous Epitaphs for GENERAL WOLFE;
    *for the best of which a Premium of L.*100 *was*
    promised.

The Muse, a shameless, mercenary jade!
Has now assumed the arch-tongued lawyer's
    trade;
In Wolfe's deserving praises silent she,
Till flattered with the prospect of a fee.

HORACE, ODE XI. LIB. I.

Ne'er fash your thumb what gods decree
To be the weird o' you or me,
Nor deal in cantrip's kittle cunning
To spier how fast your days are running;
But patient lippen for the best,
Nor be in dowy thought opprest,
Whether we see mair winters come,
Than this that spits wi' cankered foam.
Now moisten weel your geyzened wa's
Wi' couthy friends and hearty blaws;
Ne'er let your hope o'ergang your days,
For eild and thraldom never stays;
The day looks gash, toot aff your horn,
Nor care yae strae about the morn.

EPIGRAM,

On a Lawyer's desiring one of the Tribe to look with respect to a Gibbet.

THE lawyers may revere that tree,
　Where thieves so oft have strung,
Since, by the law's most wise decree,
　Her thieves are never hung.

EPIGRAM,

Written Extempore, at the Desire of a Gentleman who was rather ill-favoured, but who had a beautiful Family of Children.

SCOTT and his children emblems are
　Of real good and evil ;
His children are like cherubims,
　But Scott is like the devil.

⸻

EPILOGUE,

Spoken by Mr Wilson, *at the Theatre-Royal, in the Character of an Edinburgh Buck.*

Ye who oft finish care in Lethe's cup ;
Who love to swear, and roar, and keep it up ;
List to a brother's voice, whose sole delight
Is—sleep all day, and riot all the night.

Last night, when potent draughts of mellow
  wine
Did sober reason into wit refine ;
When lusty Bacchus had contrived to drain
The sullen vapours from our shallow brain,
We sallied forth (for valour's dazzling sun
Up to his bright meridian had run) ;
And, like renowned Quixote and his Squire,
Spoils and adventures were our sole desire.

First, we approached a seeming sober dame,
Preceded by a lanthorn's pallid flame,

Borne by a liveryed puppy's servile hand,
The slave obsequious of her stern command.—
Curse on those cits, said I, who dare disgrace
Our streets at midnight with a sober face;
Let never tallowchandler give them light,
To guide them thro' the dangers of the night.
The valet's cane we snatched; and, demme! I
Made the frail lanthorn on the pavement lie.
The guard, still watchful of the lieges' harm,
With slow paced motion stalked at the alarm.
" Guard, seize the rogues!" the angry madam
    cried,
And all the guard, with " Sieze ta rogue," re-
    plied.

   As, in a war, there's nothing judged so right
As a concerted and prudential flight:
So we, from guard and scandal to be freed,
Left them the field and burial of their dead.

   Next, we approached the bounds of George's
    Square:—
Blest place!—No watch, no constables, come
    there.
Now, had they borrowed Argus' eyes, who
    saw us,
All was made dark and desolate as chaos:

Lamps tumbled after lamps, and lost their
    lustres,
Like doomsday, when the stars shall fall in
    clusters.
Let Fancy paint what dazzling glory grew
From crystal gems, when Phœbus came in
    view :
Each shattered orb ten thousand fragments
    strews,
And a new sun in every fragment shews.

Hear then, my Bucks ! how drunken fate
    decreed us
For a nocturnal visit to the Meadows,
And how we, valorous champions ! durst en-
    gage—
O deed unequalled !—both the Bridge and Cage,
The rage of perilous winters which had stood ;—
This 'gainst the wind, and that against the
    flood :
But what nor wind, nor flood, nor heaven
    could bend e'er,
We tumbled down, my Bucks ! and made sur-
    render.

What are your far-famed warriors to us,
'Bout whom historians make such mighty fuss !
Posterity may think it was uncommon
That Troy should be demolished for a woman ;

But ours your ten years sieges will excel,
And justly be esteemed the nonpareil.
Our cause is slighter than a dame's betrothing;
For all these mighty feats have sprung from—
      nothing.

===

THE AUTHOR'S LIFE.

My life is like the flowing stream
That glides where Summer's beauties teem,
Meets all the riches of the gale,
That on its watery bosom sail,
And wanders, 'midst Elysian groves,
Thro' all the haunts that Fancy loves.

May I, when drooping days decline,
And 'gainst those genial streams combine,
The Winter's sad decay forsake,
And centre in my parent lake.

ON THE AUTHOR'S INTENTION OF GOING TO SEA.

FORTUNE and Bob, e'er since his birth,
   Could never yet agree;
She fairly kicked him from the earth,
   To try his fate at sea.

MY LAST WILL.

WHILE sober folks, in humble prose,
Estate, and goods, and gear, dispose,
A poet surely may disperse
His moveables in doggerel verse;
And, fearing death my blood will fast chill,
I hereby constitute my last will.

   Then, wit ye me to have made o'er
To Nature my poetic lore :
To her I give and grant the freedom
Of paying to the bards who need 'em

As many talents as she gave,
When I became the Muse's slave.

Thanks to the gods, who made me poor!
No lukewarm friends molest my door,
Who always shew a busy care
For being legatee or heir.
Of this stamp none will ever follow
The youth that's favoured by Apollo.

But to those few who know my case,
Nor thought a poet's friend disgrace,
The following trifles I bequeath,
And leave them with my kindest breath;
Nor will I burden them with payment,
Of debts incurred, or coffin raiment,
As yet 'twas never my intent
To pass an Irish compliment.

To JAMIE RAE*, who oft, *jocosus*,
With me partook of cheering doses,
I leave my snuff-box to regale
His senses after drowsy meal,
And wake remembrance of a friend
Who lov'd him to his latter end:
But if this pledge should make him sorry,
And argue like *memento mori*,

* Solicitor at law, and the Poet's intimate friend.

He may bequeath't 'mong stubborn fellows
To all the finer feelings callous,
Who think that parting breath's a sneeze
To set sensations all at ease.

    To OLIPHANT*, my friend, I legate
Those scrolls poetic, which he may get,
With ample freedom to correct
Those writs I ne'er could retrospect;
With power to him and his succession,
To print and sell a new impression:
And here I fix on Ossian's head
A domicil for Doric reed,
With as much power *ad Musæ bona*
As I *in propria persona*.

    To HAMILTON† I give the task
Outstanding debts to crave and ask;
And that my Muse he may not dub ill,
For loading him with so much trouble,
My debts I leave him *singulatim*,
As they are mostly *desperatim*.

    To thee, whose genius can provoke
Thy passions to the bowl or sock;

---

* Late Bookseller in Edinburgh.

† Solicitor at law, and the Poet's intimate friend.

For love to thee, Woods! and the Nine,
Be my immortal Shakespeare thine.
Here may you through the alleys turn,
Where Falstaff laughs, where heroes mourn,
And boldly catch the glowing fire
That dwells in raptures on his lyre.

Now, at my dirge (if dirge there be),
Due to the Muse and Poetry,
Let HUTCHISON* attend; for none is
More fit to guide the ceremonies:
As I, in health, with him would often
This clay-built mansion wash and soften,
So let my friends with him partake
The generous wine at dirge or wake.—

And I consent to registration
Of this my will for preservation,
That patent it may be, and seen,
In WALTER's Weekly Magazine.
Witness whereof, these presents wrote are
By William Blair, the public notar,
And, for the tremour of my hand,
Are signed by him at my command.

His
R. ✗ F.
Mark.

* A Tavern-keeper.

CODICIL

To R. Fergusson's Last Will.

WHEREAS, by testament dated blank,
Enrolled in the poetic rank,
'Midst brighter themes that weekly come.
To make parade at WALTER's Drum,
I there, for certain weighty causes,
Produced some kind bequeathing clauses,
And left to friends (as 'tis the custom
With nothing till our death to trust 'em)
Some tokens of a pure regard
From one who lived and died a bard.

   If Poverty has any crime in
Teaching mankind the art of rhyming;
Then by these presents, know all mortals
Who come within the Muse's portals,
That I approve my will aforesaid,
But think that something might be more said,

And only now would humbly seek
The liberty to add and eik
To test'ment which already made is,
And duly registered, as said is.

To TULLOCH*, who, in kind compassion,
Departed from the common fashion,
And gave to me, who never paid it,
Two flasks of port, upon my credit,
I leave the flasks, as full of air,
As his of ruddy moisture were;
Nor let him to complain begin;
He'll get no more of cat than skin.

To WALTER RUDDIMAN*, whose pen
Still screened me from the Dunce's den,
I leave of phiz a picture, saving
To him the freedom of engraving
Therefrom a copy, to embellish,
And give his work a smarter relish;
For prints and frontispieces bind do
Our eyes to stationary window,
As superfluities in clothes
Set off and signalize the beaux.
Not that I think in readers' eyes
My visage will be deemed a prize;

* A Wine-merchant.

† The Publisher of the Weekly Magazine.

But works that others would outrival,
At glaring copperplates connive all ;
And prints do well with him that led is
To shun the substance, hunt the shadows ;
For, if a picture, 'tis enough ;
A Newton, or a Jamie Duff*.
Nor would I recommend to Walter,
This scheme of copperplates to alter,
Since others at the samen prices
Propose to give a dish that nice is,
Folks will desert his ordinary,
Unless, like theirs, his dishes vary.

To WILLIAMSON†, and his resetters,
Dispersing of the burial letters,
That they may pass with little cost
Fleet on the wings of Penny-post ;
Always providing and declaring,
That Peter shall be ever sparing,
To make, as use is, the demand
For letters that may come to hand,
To me addressed while *locum tenens*
Of earth and of corporeal penance ;
Where, if he fail, it is my will,
His legacy be void and null.

* A fool who attended at funerals.

† The Penny-post Master.

Let honest GREENLAW* be the staff
On which I lean for epitaph.
And, that the Muses, at my end,
May know I had a learned friend,
Whate'er of character he's seen
In me through humour or chagrin,
I crave his genius may narrate in
The strength of Ciceronian Latin.

Reserving to myself the power
To alter this at latest hour,
Cum privilegio revocare,
Without assigning *ratio quare:*
And I (as in the Will before did)
Consent this deed shall be recorded :
In testimonium cujus rei,
These presents are delivered by
                    R. FERGUSSON.

‡ An excellent classical scholar.

SCOTS POEMS.

AN ECLOGUE.

'Twas e'ening, whan the speckled gowdspink
  sang,
Whan new-fa'en dew in blobs o' crystal hang;
Than Will and Sandie thought they'd wrought
  eneugh,
And loosed their sair-toiled owsen frae the
  pleugh:
Before they ca'd their cattle to the town,
The lads, to draw their breath, e'en sat them
  down.
To the stiff sturdy aik they leaned their backs,
While honest Sandie thus began the cracks.

SANDIE.

Yence I could hear the laverock's shrill-tuned
    throat,
And listen to the clattering gowdspink's note;
Yence I could whistle cantily as they,
To owsen, as they tilled my raggit clay;
But now I wou'd as leive maist lend my lugs
To tuneless puddocks croaking i' the bogs;
I sigh at hame, a-field am dowie too,
To sough a tune I'll never crook my mou.

WILLIE.

Foul fa' me! gif your bridal hadna been
Nae langer bygane than sin' Hallowe'en,
I could ha'e telled you but a warlock's art,
That some daft lightlyin' quean had stown your
    heart:
Our beasties here will tak their e'ening pluck;
And now, sin' Jock's gane hame the byres to
    muck,
Fain would I houp my friend will be inclined
To gi'e me a' the secrets o' his mind:
Hech, Sandie, lad! what dool's come owre ye
    now,
That you to whistle ne'er will crook your mou?

SANDIE.

Ah, Willie, Willie! I may date my wae
Frae what beted me on my bridal day;

Sair may I rue the hour in which our hands
Were knit thegither in the haly bands :
Sin that I thrave sae ill, in troth, I fancy,
Some fiend or fairy, nae sae very chancy,
Has driven me, by pawky wiles uncommon,
To wed this flytin fury of a woman.

WILLIE.

Ah! Sandie, aften hae I heard you tell,
Amang the lasses a' she bure the bell ;
And say, the modest glances o' her een
Far dang the brightest beauties o' the green ;
You ca'd her ay sae innocent, sae young,
I thought she kentna how to use her tongue.

SANDIE.

Before I married her, I'll tak my aith,
Her tongue was never louder than her breath;
But now it's turned sae souple and sae bauld,
That Job himsel cou'd scarcely thole the
scauld.

WILLIE.

Let her yelp on, be you as calm's a mouse,
Nor let your whisht be heard into the house :
Do what she can, or be as loud's she please,
Ne'er mind her flytes, but set your heart at
ease ;

Sit down and blaw your pipe, nor faush your
   thumb,
And there's my hand she'll tire, and soon sing
   dumb;
Sooner should Winter cauld confine the sea,
And lat the sma'est o' our burns rin free :
Sooner at Yule-day shall the birk be drest,
Or birds in sapless busses big their nest,
Before a tonguey woman's noisy plea
Should ever be a cause to danton me.

SANDIE.

Weel could I this abide ; but, oh! I fear,
I'll soon be twined o' a' my warldly gear.
My kirnstaff now stands gizzened at the door ;
My cheese-rack toom, that ne'er was toom
   before ;
My kye may now rin rowtin to the hill,
And on the naked yird their milkness spill ;
She seenil lays her hand upo' a turn,
Neglects the kebbuck, and forgets the kirn :
I vow, my hair-mould milk would poison dogs,
As it stands lappered i' the dirty cogs.

Before the seed, I sell't my ferra cow,
And wi' the profit coft a stane o' woo' ;
I thought, by priggin, that she might hae spun
A plaidie, light, to screen me frae the sun :

But tho' the siller's scant, the cleedin dear,
She has na ca'd about the wheel the year.
Last ouk but ane I was frae hame a day,
Buying a threave or twa o' beddin strae :
O ilka thing the woman had her will ;
Had fouth o' meal to bake and hens to kill :
But hyn awa to Edinbrough scoured she
To get a makin o' her fav'rite tea ;
And 'cause I left her na the weary clink,
She sell't the very trunchers frae my bink.

WILLIE.

Her tea ! ah, wae betide sic costly gear,
Or them that ever wad the price o't spier !
Sin my auld gutcher first the warld knew,
Fouk had na fund the Indies whare it grew.
I mind mysel, its nae sae lang sinsyne,
Whan auntie Marion did her stamack tyne,
That Davs, our gard'ner, came frae Applebog,
And gae her tea to tak by way o' drog.

SANDIE.

Whan ilka herd for cauld his fingers rubs,
And cakes o' ice are seen upo' the dubs ;
At mornin, whan frae pleugh or fauld I come,
I'll see a braw reek rising frae my lum,
And aiblins think to get a rantin blaze,
To fley the frost awa, and toast my taes ;

But whan I shoot my nose in, ten to ane
If I weelfardly see my ain hearthstane:
She round the ingle wi' her gimmers sits,
Crammin their gebbies wi' her nicest bits.
While the gudeman, out-by, maun fill his crap
Frae the milk coggie, or the parritch caup.

WILLIE.

Sandie! gif this were ony common plea,
I should the lealest o' my counsel gie;
But mak or meddle betwixt man and wife,
Is what I never did in a' my life.
Its wearing on now to the tail o' May,
And just between the bear-seed and the hay;
As lang's an orra mornin may be spared,
Stap your wa's east the haugh, and tell the
    laird:
For he's a man weel versed in a' the laws;
Kens baith their outs and ins, their cracks and
    flaws;
And ay right gleg, whan things are out o' joint,
At sattlin o' a nice or kittle point.
But yonder's Jock, he'll ca' your owsen hame,
And tak the tidings to your thrawart dame,
That ye're awa ae peacefu' meal to prie,
And tak your supper, kail or sowens, wi' me.

AN ECLOGUE,

To the Memory of Dr William Wilkie, *late Professor of Natural Philosophy in the University of St Andrews.*

GEORDIE AND DAVIE.

GEORDIE.

Blaw saft my reed, and kindly, to my maen,
Weel may ye thole a saft and dowie strain.
Nae mair to you shall shepherds, in a ring,
Wi' blithness skip, or lasses lilt and sing ;
Sic sorrow now maun sadden ilka ee ;
And ilka waefu' shepherd grieve wi' me.

DAVIE.

Wharefore begin a sad and dowie strain,
Or banish liltin frae the Fifan plain ?
Tho' Simmer's gane, and we nae langer view
The blades o' claver wat wi' pearls o' dew ;
Cauld Winter's bleakest blasts we'll eithly cour,
Our elden's driven, and our har'st is owre ;

Our rucks, fu' thick, are stackit i' the yard;
For the Yule-feast a sautit mart's prepared;
The ingle-nook supplies the simmer fields,
And aft as mony gleefu' moments yields.
Swyth, man! fling a' your sleepy springs awa,
And on your canty whistle gie's a blaw:
Blithness, I trow, maun lighten ilka ee;
And ilka canty callant sing like me.

GEORDIE.

Na, na! a canty spring wad now impart
Just threefauld sorrow to my heavy heart.
Thof to the weet my ripened aits had fa'an,
Or shake-winds owre my rigs wi' pith had blawn;
To this I could hae said, " I carena by,"
Nor fund occasion now my cheeks to dry.
Crosses like thae, or lack o' warld's gear,
Are naething, when we tyne a friend that's dear.
Ah! waes me for you, Willie! mony a day
Did I wi' you on yon broom-thackit brae
Hound aff my sheep, and let them careless gang
To harken to your cheery tale or sang;—
Sangs that, for ay, on Caledonia's strand,
Shall sit the foremost 'mang her tunefu' band.

I dreamt, yestreen, his deadly wraith I saw
Gang by my een, as white's the driven snaw;
My collie, Ringie, youfed and youled a' night;
Coured and crap nar me, in an unco fright:

I wakened, fleyed, and shook baith lith and lim'.
A cauldness took me, and my sight grew dim;
I kent that it forspake approaching wae,
Whan my poor doggie was disturbit sae.
Nae sooner did the day begin to dawn,
Than I beyont the knowe fu' speedy ran,
Whare I was keppit wi' the heavy tale
That sets ilk dowie sangster to bewail.

DAVIE.

And wha on Fifan bents can weel refuse
To gie the tear o' tribute to his muse?——
Fareweel ilk cheery spring, ilk canty note,
Be daffin and ilk idle play forgot;
Bring ilka herd the mournfu', mournfu' boughs,
Rosemary sad, and ever dreary yews;
Thae lat be steepit i' the saut, saut tear,
To weet wi' hallowed draps his sacred bier,
Whase sangs will ay in Scotland be rever'd,
While slow-gawn owsen turn the flowery swaird;
While bonny lammies lick the dews of spring,
While gaudsmen whistle, or while birdies sing.

GEORDIE.

'Twas na for weel-timed verse or sangs alane,
He bore the bell frae ilka shepherd swain.
Nature to him had gien a kindly lore,
Deep, a' her mystic ferlies to explore:

For a' her secret workings he could gie
Reasons that wi' her principles agree.
Ye saw, yoursel, how weel his mailin thrave ;
Ay better faughed and snodit than the lave :
Lang had the thristles and thè dockans been
In use to wag their taps upo' the green,
Whare now his bonny rigs delight the view,
And thrivin hedges drink the cauler dew*.

DAVIE.

They tell me, Geordie ! he had sic a gift,
That scarce a starnie blinkit frae the lift,
But he would some auld warld name for't find,
As gart him keep it freshly in his mind.
For this, some ca'd him an uncanny wight :
The clash gaed round, " he had the second
   " sight ;"
A tale that never failed to be the pride
O' grannies spinnin at the ingle-side.

GEORDIE.

But now he's gane; and Fame, that, whan alive,
Seenil lats ony o' her votaries thrive,
Will frae his shinin name a' mots withdraw,
And on her loudest trump his praises blaw.

 * Dr Wilkie had a farm near St Andrews, on which he
made great improvements.

Lang may his sacred banes untroubled rest!
Lang may his truff in gowans gay be drest!
Scholars and bards unheard of yet shall come,
And stamp memorials on his grassy tomb,
Which in yon ancient kirk-yard shall remain,
Famed as the urn that hauds the Mantuan
    swain.

===

ELEGY,

On the Death of MR DAVID GREGORY, *late
Professor of Mathematics in the University of
St Andrews.*

Now mourn, ye college masters a'!
And frae your een a tear let fa';
Famed Gregory death has ta'en awa'
       Without remeid;
The skaith ye've met wi's nae that sma',
       Sin' Gregory's dead.

The students too, will miss him sair;
To school them weel his eident care;
Now they may mourn for ever mair;
                    They hae great need:
They'll hip the maist feck o' their lear,
                    Sin' Gregory's dead.

He could, by Euclid prove, lang syne,
A ganging point compos'd a line,
By numbers too, he could divine,
                    Whan he did read,
That three times three just made up nine;
                    But now he's dead.

In Algebra weel skill'd he was,
And kent fu' weel Proportion's laws:
He could mak clear baith B's and A's
                    Wi' his lang head;
Rin owre surd roots, but cracks or flaws;
                    But now he's dead.

Weel vers'd was he in architecture,
And kent the nature o' the sector:
Upo' baith globes he weel could lecture,
                    And gar's tak heed:
O' geometry he was the Hector;
                    But now he's dead.

Sae weel's he'd fley the students a',
Whan they were skelpin at the ba':
They took leg-bail, and ran awa
      Wi' pith and speed:
We winna get a sport sae braw,
      Sin' Gregory's dead.

Great 'casion hae we a' to weep,
And cleed our skins in mourning deep,
For Gregory death will fairly keep,
      To tak his nap:
He'll till the resurrection sleep,
      As sound's a tap.

THE DAFT DAYS.

Now mirk December's dowie face
Glowrs owre the rigs wi' sour grimace,
While, thro' his *minimum* o' space
      The bleer-e'ed sun,
Wi' blinkin light and stealin' pace,
      His race doth run.

Frae naked groves nae birdie sings;
To shepherd's pipe nae hillock rings;
The breeze nae od'rous flavour brings,
      Frae Borean cave;
And dwynin Nature droops her wings,
      Wi' visage grave.

Mankind but scanty pleasure glean
Frae snawy hill or barren plain,
Whan Winter, 'midst his nippin' train,
      Wi' frozen spear,
Sends drift owre a' his bleak domain,
      And guides the weir.

Auld Reikie! thou'rt the canty hole;
A bield for mony a cauldrife soul,
Wha snugly at thine ingle loll,
      Baith warm and couth;
While round they gar the bicker roll,
      To weet their mouth.

Whan merry Yule-day comes, I trow,
You'll scantlins find a hungry mou;
Sma' are our cares, our stamacks fou
      O' gusty gear,
And kickshaws, strangers to our view
      Sin' fairn-year.

Ye browster wives! now busk ye braw,
And fling your sorrows far awa ;
Then, come and gie's the tither blaw
     O' reaming ale,
Mair precious than the Well o' Spa,
      Our hearts to heal.

Then, tho' at odds wi' a' the warl',
Amang oursels we'll never quarrel ;
Tho' Discord gie a canker'd snarl,
      To spoil our glee,
As lang's there's pith into the barrel,
      We'll drink and gree.

Fiddlers ! your pins in temper fix,
And roset weel your fiddlesticks ;
But banish vile Italian tricks
      Frae out your quorum ;
Nor fortes wi' pianos mix ;—
      Gie's Tullochgorum.

For nought can cheer the heart sae weel,
As can a canty Highland reel ;
It even vivifies the heel
      To skip and dance :
Lifeless is he wha canna feel
      Its influence.

Let mirth abound ; let social cheer
Invest the dawnin' o' the year ;
Let blithesome Innocence appear,
           To crown our joy :
Nor Envy, wi' sarcastic sneer,
           Our bliss destroy.

And thou, great god of *Aquavitæ !*
Wha sways the empire o' this city ;—
Whan fou, we're sometimes capernoity ;—
           Be thou prepar'd
To hedge us frae that black banditti,
           The City Guard.

THE KING'S BIRTH-DAY

In Edinburgh.

Oh ! qualis hurly-burly fuit, si forte vidisses.
POLEMO-MIDDINIA.

I SING the day sae aften sung,
Wi' which our lugs hae yearly rung,
In whase loud praise the Muse has dung
        A' kind o' print ;
But vow ! the limmer's fairly flung ;
        There's naething in't.

I'm fain to think the joys the same
In London town as here at hame,
Whare fouk of ilka age and name,
        Baith blind and cripple,
Forgather aft, O fy for shame !
        To drink and tipple.

O Muse, be kind, and dinna fash us
To flee awa beyont Parnassus,
Nor seek for Helicon to wash us,
            That heath'nish spring;
Wi' Highland whisky scour our hawses,
            And gar us sing.

Begin then, dame, ye've drunk your fill,
You wadna hae the tither gill?
You'll trust me, mair wad do you ill,
            And ding you doitet;
Troth 'twould be sair against my will
            To hae the wyte o't.

Sing then, how, on the fourth of June,
Our bells screed aff a loyal tune,
Our ancient castle shoots at noon,
            Wi' flag-staff buskit,
Frae which the soldier blades come down
            To cock their musket.

Oh willawins! Mons Meg, for you,
'Twas firing crack'd thy muckle mou;
What black mishanter gart ye spew
            Baith gut and ga'?
I fear they bang'd thy belly fu'
            Against the law.

Right seldom am I gi'en to bannin,
But, by my saul, ye was a cannon,
Cou'd hit a man, had he been stannin
          In shire o' Fife
Sax lang Scots miles ayont Clackmannan,
          And tak his life.

The hills in terror wad cry out,
And echo to thy dinsome rout;
The herds wad gather in their nowt,
          That glowr'd wi' wonder,
Haflins afraid to bide thereout
          To hear thy thunder.

Sing likewise, Muse, how blue-gown bodies,
Like scar-craws new ta'en down frae woodies,
Come here to cast their clouted duddies,
          And get their pay:
Than them what magistrate mair proud is
          On king's birth-day?

On this great day the city-guard,
In military art weel lear'd,
Wi' powder'd pow and shaven beard,
          Gang thro' their functions,
By hostile rabble seldom spar'd
          Of clarty unctions.

O soldiers ! for your ain dear sakes,
For Scotland's, *alias* Land of Cakes,
Gie not her bairns sic deadly pakes,
   Nor be sae rude,
Wi' firelock or Lochaber ax,
   As spill their blude.

Now round and round the serpents whizz,
Wi' hissing wrath and angry phiz ;
Sometimes they catch a gentle gizz,
   Alake the day !
And singe, wi' hair-devouring bizz,
   Its curls away.

Shou'd th' owner patiently keek round,
To view the nature of his wound,
Dead pussie, dragled through the pond,
   Taks him a lounder,
Which lays his honour on the ground
   As flat's a flounder.

The Muse maun also now implore
Auld wives to steek ilk hole and bore ;
If baudrins slip but to the door,
   I fear, I fear,
She'll no lang shank upon all four
   This time o' year.

Next day each hero tells his news
O' crackit crowns and broken brows,
And deeds that here forbid the Muse
   Her theme to swell,
Or time mair precious abuse
   Their crimes to tell.

She'll rather to the fields resort,
Whare music gars the day seem short,
Whare doggies play, and lammies sport
   On gowany braes,
Whare peerless Fancy hauds her court,
   And tunes her lays.

CALLER OYSTERS.

Happy the man, who, free from care and strife,
In silken or in leathern purse retains
A splendid shilling.   He nor hears with pain
New oysters cry'd, nor sighs for cheerful ale.

PHILLIPS.

O' a' the waters that can hobble,
A fishing yole or sa'mon coble,
And can reward the fisher's trouble,
      Or south or north,
There's nane sae spacious and sae noble,
      As Firth o' Forth.

In her the skate and codlin sail ;
The eel, fu' souple, wags her tail ;
Wi' herrin, fleuk, and mackarel,
      And whytens dainty :
Their spindleshanks the labsters trail,
      Wi' partans plenty.

Auld Reikie's sons blythe faces wear;
September's merry month is near,
That brings in Neptune's caller cheer,
   New oysters fresh;
The halesomest and nicest gear
   O' fish or flesh.

O! then we needna gie a plack
For dand'ring mountebank or quack,
Wha o' their drogs sae bauldly crack,
   An' spread sic notions,
As gar their feckless patients tak
   Their stinking potions.

Come, prie, frail man! for gin thou art sick,
The oyster is a rare cathartic,
As ever doctor patient gart lick,
   To cure his ails;
Whether you hae the head or heart-ake,
   It ay prevails.

Ye tipplers, open a' your poses:
Ye, wha are fash'd wi' plouky noses,
Fling o'er your craig sufficient doses;
   You'll thole a hunder,
To fleg awa your simmer roses,
   And naething under.

Whan big as burns the gutters rin,
Gin ye hae catcht a droukit skin,
To luckie Middlemist's loup in,
        And sit fu' snug
Owre oysters and a dram o' gin,
        Or haddock lug.

Whan auld Saunt Giles, at eight o'clock,
Gars merchant lowns their shopies lock,
There we adjourn wi' hearty fouk
        To birle our bodles,
And get wharewi' to crack our joke,
        And clear our noddles.

Whan Phœbus did his winnocks steek,
How aften at that ingle cheek
Did I my frosty fingers beek,
        And prie good fare ?
I trow there was nae hame to seek,
        Whan steghin there.

While glaikit fools, owre rife o' cash,
Pamper their wames wi' fousom trash,
I think a chiel may gayly pass,
        He's nae ill bodden,
That gusts his gab wi' oyster sauce,
        An' hen weel sodden.

At Musselbrough, and eke Newhaven,
The fisher wives will get top livin'
Whan lads gang out on Sunday's even
   To treat their joes,
And tak o' fat pandores a prievin',
   Or mussel brose.

Then, sometimes, ere they flit their doup,
They'll aiblins a' their siller coup
For liquor clear, frae cutty stoup,
   To weet their wizzen,
And swallow owre a dainty soup,
   For fear they gizzen.

A' ye wha canna stand sae sicker,
Whan twice ye've toom'd the big-ars'd bicker,
Mix cauler oysters wi' your liquor,
   And I'm your debtor,
If greedy priest or drowthy vicar
   Will thole it better.

BRAID CLAITH.

Ye wha are fain to hae your name
Wrote i' the bonny book o' Fame,
Let merit nae pretension claim
   To laurell'd wreath,
But hap ye weel, baith back and wame,
   In gude Braid Claith.

He that some ells o' this may fa',
And slae-black hat on pow like snaw,
Bids bauld to bear the gree awa,
   Wi' a' this graith,
Whan bienly clad wi' shell fu' braw
   O' gude Braid Claith.

Waesuck for him wha has nae feck o't!
For he's a gowk they're sure to geck at,
A chiel that ne'er will be respeckit
   While he draws breath,
Till his four quarters are bedeckit
   Wi' gude Braid Claith.

On Sabbath-days the barber spark,
Whan he has done wi' scrapin wark,
Wi' siller broachie in his sark,
    Gangs trigly, faith!
Or to the Meadow, or the Park,
    In gude Braid Claith.

Weel might ye trow, to see them there,
That they to shave your haffits bare,
Or curl and sleek a pickle hair,
    Wad be right laith,
Whan pacing wi' a gawsy air
    In gude Braid Claith.

If ony mettl'd stirrah green
For favour frae a lady's een,
He maunna care for being seen
    Before he sheath
His body in a scabbard clean
    O' gude Braid Claith.

For, gin he come wi' coat thread-bare,
A feg for him she winna care,
But crook her bonny mou' fu' sair,
    And scald him baith.
Wooers should ay their travel spare
    Without Braid Claith.

Braid Claith lends fouk an unco heese,
Maks mony kail-worms butterflies,
Gies mony a doctor his degrees
    For little skaith :
In short, you may be what you please
     Wi' gude Braid Claith.

For thof ye had as wise a snout on
As Shakespeare or Sir Isaac Newton,
Your judgment fouk wad hae a doubt on,
    I'll tak my aith,
Till they cou'd see ye wi' a suit on
     O' gude Braid Claith.

ELEGY,

On the DEATH *of* SCOTS MUSIC.

Mark it Cæsario; it is old and plain,
The spinsters and the knitters in the sun,
And the free maids that weave their thread with bones,
Do use to chant it.

SHAKESPEARE'S TWELFTH NIGHT.

On Scotia's plains, in days of yore,
When lads and lasses tartan wore,
Saft Music rang on ilka shore,
   In hamely weed ;
But Harmony is now no more,
   And Music dead.

Round her the feather'd choir wad wing,
Sae bonnily she wont to sing,
And sleely wake the sleeping string,
   Their sang to lead,
Sweet as the zephyrs of the spring ;
   But now she's dead.

Mourn ilka nymph and ilka swain,
Ilk sunny hill and dowie glen;
Let weeping streams and Naiads drain
   Their fountain head;
Let Echo swell the dolefu' strain,
   Since Music's dead.

Whan the saft vernal breezes ca'
The grey-hair'd Winter's fogs awa',
Naebody then is heard to blaw,
   Near hill or mead,
On chaunter, or on aiten straw,
   Since Music's dead.

Nae lasses now, on simmer days,
Will lilt at bleaching o' their claes;
Nae herds on Yarrow's bonny braes,
   Or banks o' Tweed,
Delight to chant their hameil lays,
   Since Music's dead.

At gloamin now the bagpipe's dumb,
Whan weary owsen hameward come;
Sae sweetly as it wont to bum,
   And pibrachs skreed;
We never hear its warlike hum;
   For Music's dead.

Macgibbon's gane: Ah! waes my heart!
The man in Music maist expert,
Wha could sweet melody impart,
       And tune the reed,
Wi' sic a slee and pawky art;
        But now he's dead.

Ilk carline now may grunt and grane,
Ilk bonny lassie mak great mane,
Since he's awa', I trow there's nane
       Can fill his stead;
The blithest sangster on the plain!
        Alake, he's dead!

Now foreign sonnets bear the gree,
And crabbed queer variety
Of sounds fresh sprung frae Italy,
       A bastard breed!
Unlike that saft-tongu'd melody
        Which now lies dead.

Could lav'rocks at the dawning day,
Could linties chirming frae the spray,
Or todling burns that smoothly play
       O'er gowden bed,
Compare wi' Birks of Invermay?
        But now they're dead.

O Scotland ! that could aince afford
To bang the pith of Roman sword,
Winna your sons, wi' joint accord,
         To battle speed ?
And fight till Music be restor'd,
         Which now lies dead.

HALLOW-FAIR.

At Hallowmas, whan nights grow lang,
  And starnies shine fu' clear,
Whan fouk, the nippin' cauld to bang,
  Their winter hap-warms wear,
Near Edinbrough a fair there hauds,
  I wat there's nane whase name is,
For strappin dames and sturdy lads,
  And cap and stoup, mair famous
         Than it that day.

Upo' the tap o' ilka lum
  The sun began to keek,
And bade the trig-made maidens come
  A sightly joe to seek

At Hallow-fair, whare browsters rare
   Keep gude ale on the gantries,
And dinna scrimp ye o' a skair
   O' kebbucks frae their pantries,
          Fu' saut that day.

Here country John, in bannet blue,
   And eke his Sunday's claes on,
Rins after Meg wi' rokelay new,
   And sappy kisses lays on :
She'll tauntin' say, " Ye silly coof!
   " Be o' your gab mair spairin' ;"
He'll tak the hint, and criesh her loof
   Wi' what will buy her fairin',
          To chow that day.

Here chapmen billies tak their stand,
   And shaw their bonny wallies ;
Wow ! but they lie fu' gleg aff hand
   To trick the silly fallows :
Heh, sirs ! what cairds and tinklers come,
   And ne'er-do-weel horse-coupers,
And spae-wives, fenzying to be dumb,
   Wi' a' siclike landloupers,
          To thrive that day !

Here Sawney cries, frae Aberdeen,
   " Come ye to me fa need ;

" The brawest shanks that e'er were seen
 " I'll sell ye cheap an' guid :
" I wyt they are as protty hose
 " As come frae weyr or leem :
" Here, tak a rug, and shaw's your pose ;
 " Forseeth, my ain's but teem
    And light this day."

Ye wives, as ye gang through the fair,
 O mak your bargains hooly !
O' a' thir wylie louns beware,
 Or, fegs ! they will ye spulzie.
For, fairnyear, Meg Thamson got,
 Frae thir mischievous villains,
A scaw'd bit o' a penny note,
 That lost a score o' shillins
    To her that day.

The dinlin drums alarm our ears ;
 The sergeant screechs fu' loud,
" A' gentlemen and volunteers
 " That wish your country gude,
" Come here to me, and I sall gie
 " Twa guineas and a crown ;
" A bowl o' punch, that, like the sea,
 " Will soom a lang dragoon
    " Wi' ease this day."

Without, the cuissars prance and nicker,
　　And owre the ley-rig scud ;
In tents, the carles bend the bicker,
　　And rant and roar like wud.
Then there's sic yellowchin and din,
　　Wi' wives and wee-anes gabblin,
That ane might trow they were a-kin
　　To a' the tongues at Babylon,
　　　　　　　　Confus'd that day.

Whan Phœbus ligs in Thetis' lap,
　　Auld Reikie gies them shelter,
Whare cadgily they kiss the cap,
　　And ca't round helter-skelter.
Jock Bell gaed furth to play his freaks ;
　　Great cause he had to rue it ;
For frae a stark Lochaber ax
　　He gat a clamihewit
　　　　　　　　Fu' sair that night.

" Ohon ! (quo' he), I'd rather be
　" By sword or bagnet stickit,
" Than hae my crown or body wi'
　" Sic deadly weapons nickit."
Wi' that he gat anither straik
　　Mair weighty than before,
That gart his feckless body aik,
　　And spew the reekin gore
　　　　　　　　Fu' red that night.

He pechin on the cawsey lay,
  O' kicks and cuffs weel sair'd ;
A Highland aith the sergeant gae,
  " She maun pe see our guard."
Out spak the weirlike corporal,
  " Bring in ta drucken sot :"
They trail'd him ben, and by my saul,
  He paid his drucken groat
          For that neist day.

Gude fouk, as ye come frae the fair,
  Bide yont frae this black squad ;
There's nae sic savages elsewhere
  Allow'd to wear cockade.
Than the strong lion's hungry maw,
  Or tusk o' Russian bear,
Frae their wanruly fellin paw
  Mair cause ye hae to fear
          Your death that day.

A wee soup drink does unco weel,
  To haud the heart aboon ;
It's gude, as lang's a canny chiel
  Can stand steeve in his shoon.
But, gin a birkie's owre weel sair'd,
  It gars him aften stammer
To pleys that bring him to the guard,
  And eke the council-chaumir,
          Wi' shame that day.

ODE TO THE BEE.

HERDS ! blithesome tune your canty reeds,
And welcome to the gowany meads
The pride o' a' the insect thrang,
A stranger to the green sae lang.
Unfauld ilk buss, and ilka brier,
The bounties o' the gleesome year,
To Him whase voice delights the spring ;
Whase soughs the saftest slumbers bring.
    The trees in simmer cleedin drest,
The hillocks in their greenest vest,
The brawest flow'rs rejoic'd we see
Disclose their sweets, and ca' on thee,
Blithely to skim on wanton wing
Thro' a' the fairy haunts o' Spring.
    Whan fields hae gat their dewy gift,
And dawnin breaks upo' the lift,
Then gang your wa's thro' hight and howe,
Seek caller haugh or sunny knowe,
Or ivy craig, or burn-bank brae,
Whare Industry shall bid you gae,

For hiney, or for waxen store,
To ding sad poortith frae the door.

    Cou'd feckless creature, man, be wise,
The simmer o' his life to prize,
In winter he might fend fu' bauld,
His eild unkend to nippin cauld;
Yet thir, alas! are antrin fouk,
Wha lade their scape wi' winter stock.
Auld age maist feckly glowrs right dour
Upo' the ailings o' the poor,
Wha houp for nae comforting, save
That dowie, dismal house, the grave.
Then, feeble man, be wise; tak tent
How Industry can fetch content:
Behold the bees whare'er they wing,
Or thro' the bonny bowers o' Spring,
Whare vi'lets or whare roses blaw,
And siller dew-drops nightly fa',
Or whan on open bent they're seen,
On hether hill or thristle green;
The hiney's still as sweet that flows
Frae thristle cauld, or kendlin rose.

    Frae this the human race may learn
Reflection's hiney'd draps to earn,
Whether they tramp life's thorny way,
Or thro' the sunny vineyard stray.

    Instructive bee! attend me still;
Owre a' my labours sey your skill:

For thee shall hineysuckles rise,
Wi' ladin to your busy thighs,
And ilka shrub surround my cell,
Whareon ye like to hum and dwell:
My trees in bourachs owre my ground
Shall fend ye frae ilk blast o' wind:
Nor e'er shall herd, wi' ruthless spike,
Delve out the treasures frae your bike,
But in my fence be safe, and free
To live, and work, and sing, like me.

   Like thee, by Fancy wing'd, the Muse
Scuds ear' and heartsome owre the dews,
Fu' vogie, and fu' blithe to crap
The winsome flowers frae Nature's lap,
Twinin her livin garlands there,
That lyart Time can ne'er impair.

ON SEEING A

BUTTERFLY IN THE STREET.

Daft gowk, in macaroni dress,
Are ye come here to shaw your face,
Bowden wi' pride o' simmer gloss,
To cast a dash at Reikie's cross ;
And glowr at mony a twa-legg'd creature,
Flees, braw by art, tho' worms by nature?

  Like country laird in city cleeding,
Ye're come to town to lear' good breeding ;
To bring ilk darling toast and fashion
In vogue amang the flee creation,
That they, like buskit belles and beaux,
May crook their mou' fu' sour at those
Whase weird is still to creep, alas !
Unnotic'd 'mang the humble grass ;
While you, wi' wings new buskit trim,
Can far frae yird and reptiles skim ;
Newfangle grown wi' new-got form,
You soar aboon your mither worm.

Kind Nature lent but for a day
Her wings to mak ye sprush and gay ;
In her habuliments a while
Ye may your former sell beguile,
And ding awa' the vexing thought
O' hourly dwinin' into nought,
By beengin' to your foppish brithers,
Black corbies dress'd in peacock's feathers ;
Like thee they dander here and there,
Whan Simmer's blinks are warm and fair,
And lo'e to snuff the healthy balm,
Whan E'enin' spreads her wing sae calm ;
But whan she girns and glow'rs sae dour
Frae Borean houff in angry show'r,
Like thee they scour frae street or field,
And hap them in a lyther bield ;
For they were never made to dree
The adverse gloom o' Fortune's e'e,
Nor ever pried life's pinin' woes,
Nor pu'd the prickles wi' the rose.

Poor Butterfly ! thy case I mourn,
To green kail-yard and fruits return :
How could you troke the mavis' note
For " penny pies all-pipin' hot ?"
Can lintie's music be compar'd
Wi' gruntles frae the City Guard ?
Or can our flow'rs, at ten hour's bell,
The gowan or the spink excel ?

Now shou'd our sclates wi' hailstanes ring,
What cabbage-fauld wad screen your wing;
Say, fluttering fairy! wert thy hap
To light beneath braw Nanny's cap,
Wad she, proud butterfly of May!
In pity let you skaithless gae?
The furies glancing frae her een
Wad rug your wings o' siller sheen,
That, wae for thee! far, far outvy
Her Paris artist's finest dye;
Then a' your bonny spraings wad fall,
And you a worm be left to crawl.

To sic mishanter rins the laird
Wha quits his ha'-house and kail-yard,
Grows politician, scours to court,
Whare he's the laughing-stock and sport
O' Ministers, wha jeer and jibe,
And heeze his hopes wi' thought o' bribe,
Till in the end they flae him bare,
Leave him to poortith, and to care.
Their fleetchin' words owre late he sees,
He trudges hame, repines, and dies.

Sic be their fa' wha dirk their ben
In blackest business nae their ain;
And may they scad their lips fu' leal,
That dip their spoons in ither's kail.

ODE TO THE GOWDSPINK.

FRAE fields where Spring her sweets has blawn
Wi' caller verdure owre the lawn,
The Gowdspink comes in new attire,
The brawest 'mang the whistling choir,
That, ere the sun can clear his een,
Wi' glib notes sane the Simmer's green.

Sure Nature herried mony a tree,
For spraings and bonny spats to thee:
Nae mair the rainbow can impart
Sic glowin ferlies o' her art,
Whase pencil wrought its freaks at will
On thee, the sey-piece o' her skill.
Nae mair thro' straths in Simmer dight
We seek the rose to bless our sight;
Or bid the bonny wa'-flowers sprout
On yonder ruin's lofty snout.
Thy shinin garments far outstrip
The cherries upo' Hebe's lip,
And fool the tints that Nature chose
To busk and paint the crimson rose.

'Mang men, wae's heart! we aften find
The brawest drest want peace o' mind,
While he that gangs wi' ragged coat
Is weel contentit wi' his lot.
Whan wand wi' glewy birdlime's set,
To steal far aff your dautit mate,
Blithe wad ye change your cleeding gay
In lieu of lav'rock's sober gray.
In vain thro' woods you sair may ban
The envious treachery of man,
That wi' your gowden glister ta'en,
Still hunts you on the Simmer's plain,
And traps you 'mang the sudden fa's
O' Winter's dreary, dreepin snaws.
Now steekit frae the gowany field,
Frae ilka fav'rite houff and beild;
But mergh, alas! to disengage
Your bonny buik frae fettering cage,
Your free-born bosom beats in vain
For darling liberty again.
In window hung, how aft we see
Thee keek around at warblers free,
That carol saft, and sweetly sing
Wi' a' the blitheness o' the Spring?
Like Tantalus they hing you here
To spy the glories o' the year;
And tho' you're at the burnie's brink,
They douna suffer you to drink.

Ah, Liberty! thou bonny dame,
How wildly wanton is thy stream
Round whilk the birdies a' rejoice,
And hail you wi' a gratefu' voice.
The Gowdspink chatters joyous here,
And courts wi' gleesome sangs his peer:
The mavis frae the new-bloom'd thorn
Begins his lauds at earest morn;
And herd lowns loupin o'er the grass,
Need far less fleetchin to their lass,
Than paughty damsels bred at courts,
Wha thraw their mou's, and tak the dorts;
But, reft of thee, fient flee we care
For a' that life ahint can spare.
The Gowdspink, that sae lang has kend
Thy happy sweets (his wonted friend),
Her sad confinement ill can brook
In some dark chaumer's dowie nook;
Tho' Mary's hand his nebb supplies,
Unkend to hunger's painfu' cries,
Ev'n beauty canna chear the heart
Frae life, frae liberty apart;
For now we tyne its wonted lay,
Sae lightsome, sweet, sae blithely gay.

Thus Fortune aft a curse can gie,
To wyle us far frae liberty;
Then tent her syren smiles wha list,
I'll ne'er envy your girnel's grist;

For whan fair Freedom smiles nae mair,
Care I for life? Shame fa' the hair;
A field o'ergrown wi' rankest stubble,
The essence o' a paltry bubble.

<hr>

CAULER WATER.

WHAN father Aidie first pat spade in
The bonny yard of ancient Eden,
His amry had nae liquor laid in,
      To fire his mou',
Nor did he thole his wife's upbraidin,
      For being fu'.

A cauler burn o' siller sheen,
Ran cannily out-owre the green;
And whan our gutcher's drouth had been
      To bide right sair,
He loutit down, and drank bedeen
      A dainty skair.

His bairns had a', before the flood,
A langer tack o' flesh and blood;

And on mair pithy shanks they stood
   Than Noah's line,
Wha still hae been a feckless brood,
   Wi' drinkin wine.

The fuddlin bardies, now-a-days,
Rin maukin-mad in Bacchus' praise;
And limp and stoiter thro' their lays
   Anacreontic,
While each his sea of wine displays,
   As big's the Pontic.

My Muse will no gang far frae hame,
Or scour a' airths to hound for fame;
In troth the jillet ye might blame
   For thinking on't,
Whan eithly she can find the theme
   O' *aquafont*.

This is the name that doctors use,
Their patients' noddles to confuse;
Wi' simples clad in terms abstruse,
   They labour still,
In kittle words to gar you roose
   Their want o' skill.

But we'll hae nae sic clitter-clatter;
And, briefly to expound the matter,

It shall be ca'd gude Cauler Water;
   Than whilk, I trow,
Few drugs in doctors' shops are better
   For me or you.

Tho' joints be stiff as ony rung,
Your pith wi' pain be sairly dung,
Be you in Caller Water flung
   Out o'er the lugs,
'Twill mak ye souple, swack, and young,
   Withouten drugs.

Tho' cholic or the heart-scad teaze us,
Or ony inward dwaam should seize us,
It masters a' sic fell diseases,
   That wad ye spulzie,
And brings them to a canny crisis
   Wi' little tulzie.

Wer't na for it the bonny lasses
Wad glow'r nae mair in keekin glasses,
And soon tine dint o' a' the graces
   That aft conveen
In gleefu' looks and bonny faces,
   To catch our een.

The fairest then might die a maid,
And Cupid quit his shooting trade,

For wha thro' clarty masquerade
    Cou'd then discover,
Whether the features under shade
    Were worth a lover ?

As Simmer rains bring Simmer flowers,
And leaves to cleed the birken bowers,
Sae beauty gets by cauler showers,
    Sae rich a bloom,
As for estate, or heavy dowers,
    Aft stands in room.

What maks Auld Reikie's dames sae fair ?
It cannot be the halesome air,
But cauler burn, beyond compare,
    The best o' ony,
That gars them a' sic graces skair,
    And blink sae bonny.

On May-day, in a fairy ring,
We've seen them round St Anthon's spring,
Frae grass the cauler dew-draps wring
    To weet their een,
And water clear as crystal spring,
    To synd them clean.

O may they still pursue the way,
To look sae feat, sae clean, sae gay !

Then shall their beauties glance like May,
   And, like her, be
The Goddess of the vocal spray,
   The Muse, and me.

———

THE SITTING OF THE SESSION.

PHŒBUS, sair cow'd wi' Simmer's hight,
Cours near the yird wi' blinkin light;
Cauld shaw the haughs, nae mair bedight
   Wi' Simmer's claes,
Which heese the heart o' dowie wight
   That thro' them gaes.

Weel loes me o' you, Business! now;
For ye'll weet mony a drouthy mou,
That's lang a geyzenin gane for you,
   Withouten fill
O' dribbles frae the gude brown cow,
   Or Highland gill.

The Court o' Session, weel wat I,
Pits ilk chiel's whittle i' the pye;

Can criesh the slaw-gaun wheels whan dry,
   Till Session's done ;
Tho' they'll gie mony a cheep and cry,
   Or twalt o' June.

Ye benders a', that dwall in joot,
You'll tak your liquor clean cap out ;
Synd your mouse-wabs wi' reamin stout,
   While ye hae cash,
And gar your cares a' tak the rout,
   And thumb ne'er fash.

Rob Gibb's grey giz, new-frizzled fine,
Will white as ony snaw-ba' shine ;
Weel does he loe the lawen coin,
   Whan dossied down
For whisky gills, or dribs o' wine,
   In cauld forenoon.

Bar-keepers, now, at outer door,
Tak tent as fouk gang back and fore ;
The fient ane there but pays his score ;
   Nane wins toll-free ;
Tho' ye've a cause the House before,
   Or agent be.

Gin ony, here, wi' canker knocks,
And has na lows'd his siller pocks,

Ye needna think to fleetch or cox ;—
       " Come, shaw's your gear :—
" Ae scabbit yowe spills twenty flocks :—
       " Ye's no be here."

Now, at the door they'll raise a plea :—
Crack on, my lads ! for flytin's free ;
For gin ye shou'd tongue-tackit be,
       The mair's the pity,
When scauldin but and ben we see,
       Pendente lite

The lawyers' shelfs, and printers' presses,
Grain unco sair wi' weighty cases ;
The clerk in toil his pleasure places,
       To thrive bedeen :
At five hours' bell scribes shaw their faces,
       And rake their een.

The country fouk to lawyers crook :—
" Ah, weels me o' your bonny buik !
" The benmost part o' my kist-nook
       " I'll ripe for thee,
" And willin ware my hindmost rook
       " For my decree."

But Law's a draw-wall unco deep,
Withouten rim fouk out to keep ;
       M m

A donnart chiel, whan drunk, may dreep
    Fu' sleely in,
But finds the gate baith stey and steep,
    Ere out he win.

THE RISING OF THE SESSION.

To a' men livin be it kend,
The Session now is at an end:
Writers, your finger nebs unbend,
    And quat the pen,
Till Time, wi' lyart pow, shall send
    Blithe June again.

Tir'd o' the law, and a' its phrases,
The wylie writers, rich as Crœsus,
Hurl frae the town in hackney chaises,,
    For country cheer:
The powny, that in spring-time grazes,
    Thrives a' the year.

Ye lawyers, bid fareweel to lies :—
Fareweel to din ;—fareweel to fees :—

The canny hours o' rest may please,
   Instead o' siller :
Hain'd mu'ter hauds the mill at ease,
   And fends the miller.

Blithe may they be wha wanton play
In Fortune's bonny blinkin ray :
Fu' weel can they ding dool away,
   Wi' comrades couthy,
And never dree a hungert day,
   Or e'enn drouthy.

Ohon the day ! for him that's laid
In dowie Poortith's cauldrife shade ;
Aiblins owre honest for his trade,
   He racks his wits
How he may get his buik weel clad,
   And fill his guts.

The farmers' sons, as yap as sparrows,
Are glad, I trow, to flee the barras,
And whistle to the pleugh and harrows,
   At barley seed :
What writer wadna gang as far as
   He cou'd for bread ?

After their yokin', I wat weel,
They'll stoo the kebbuck to the heel ;

Eith can the pleugh-stilts gar a chiel
   Be unco vogie,
Clean to lick aff his crowdie-meal,
   And scart his cogie.

Now mony a fallow's dung adrift
To a' the blasts beneath the lift ;
And tho' their stamack's aft in tift,
   In vacance time,
Yet seenil do they ken the rift
   O' stappit wame.

Now, gin a notar shou'd be wanted,
You'll find the pillars gayly planted :
For little thing protests are granted
   Upo' a bill,
And weightiest matters covenanted
   For half a gill.

Naebody taks a mornin drib
O' Holland gin frae Robin Gibb ;
And, tho' a dram to Rob's mair sib,
   Than is his wife,
He maun tak time to daut his rib,
   Till siller's rife.

This vacance is a heavy doom
On Indian Peter's coffee-room ;

For a' his china pigs are toom;
   Nor do we see
In wine the soucker biskets soum,
   As light's a flee.

But stop, my Muse! nor mak a mane;
Pate does na fend on that alane;
He can fell twa dogs wi' ae bane,
   While ither fouk
Maun rest themsels content wi' ane,
   Nor farer trock.

Ye changehouse-keepers, never grumble;
Tho' you a while your bickers whumble,
Be unco patientfu' and humble,
   Nor mak a din,
Tho' good joot binna kend to rumble
   Your wame within.

You needna grudge to draw your breath
For little mair than half a reath;
Then, gin we a' be spar'd frae death,
   We'll gladly prie
Fresh noggans o' your reamin graith
   Wi' blithesome glee.

LEITH RACES.

In July month, ae bonny morn
  Whan Nature's rokelay green
Was spread owre ilka rig o' corn,
  To charm our rovin een ;
Glowrin about, I saw a quean,
  The fairest 'neath the lift :
Her een were o' the siller sheen ;
  Her skin, like snawy drift,
              Sae white that day.

Quo' she, " I ferly unco sair,
  " That ye sud musin gae ;
" Ye wha hae sung o' Hallow-fair,
  " Her Winter's pranks, and play ;
" Whan on Leith-sands the racers rare
  " Wi' Jocky louns are met,
" Their orra pennies there to ware,
  " And drown themsels in debt
              Fu' deep that day."

And wha are ye, my winsome dear,
   That taks the gate sae early ?
Whare do ye win, gin ane may speer ;
   For I right meikle ferly,
That sic braw buskit laughin lass
   Thir bonny blinks shou'd gie,
And loup, like Hebe, owre the grass,
   As wanton, and as free
               Frae dool this day ?

" I dwall amang the cauler springs
   " That weet the Land o' Cakes,
" And aften tune my canty strings
   " At bridals and late-wakes.
" They ca' me MIRTH :—I ne'er was kend
   " To grumble or look sour ;
" But blithe wad be a lift to lend,
   " Gif ye wad sey my power,
               And pith, this day."

A bargain be't ; and by my fegs !
   Gif ye will be my mate,
Wi' you I'll screw the cheery pegs ;
   Ye shanna find me blate :
We'll reel and ramble thro' the sands,
   And jeer wi' a' we meet ;
Nor hip the daft and gleesome bands
   That fill Edina's street
               Sae thrang this day.

Ere servant-maids had wont to rise
    To seethe the breakfast kettle,
Ilk dame her brawest ribbons tries,
    To put her on her mettle,
Wi' wiles some silly chiel to trap,
    (And troth he's fain to get her);
But she'll craw kniefly in his crap,
    Whan, wow! he canna flit her
              Frae hame that day.

Now, mony a scaw'd and bare-ars'd loun
    Rise early to their wark :
Enough to fley a muckle town,
    Wi' dinsome squeel and bark.
" Here is the true and faithfu' list
    " O' Noblemen and Horses ;
" Their eild, their weight, their height,
      " their grist,
    " That rin for plates or purses,
              " Fu' fleet this day."

To whisky plouks that brunt for ouks
    On town-guard sodgers' faces,
Their barber bauld his whittle crooks
    And scrapes them for the races.
Their stumps, erst used to philibegs,
    Are dight in spatterdashes,
Whase barkent hides scarce fend their legs
    Frae weet and weary plashes
              O' dirt that day.

" Come, hafe a care (the Captain cries),
  " On guns your bagnets thraw ;
" Now mind your manual exercise,
  " And marsh down raw by raw."
And as they march, he'll glowr about,
  'Tent a' their cuts and scars :
'Mang them fell mony a gawsy snout
  Has gusht in birth-day wars,
               Wi' blude that day.

Her nainsel maun be carefu' now,
  Nor maun she be mislear'd,
Sin baxters lads hae seal'd a vow,
  To skelp and clout the guard.
I'm sure Auld Reikie kens o' nane
  That wad be sorry at it,
Tho' they should dearly pay the kain,
  And get their tails weel sautit,
               And sair, thir days.

The tinkler billies i' the Bow,
  Are now less eident clinkin ;
As lang's their pith or siller dow,
  They're daffin and they're drinkin.
Bedown Leith Walk, what burrachs reel,
  O' ilka trade and station,
That gar their wives and childer feel
  Toom wames, for their libation
               O' drink thir days !

The browster wives thegither harl
  A' trash that they can fa' on ;
They rake the grunds o' ilka barrel,
  To profit by the lawen :
For weel wat they, a skin leal het
  For drinkin needs nae hire ;
At drumbly gear they tak nae pet ;
  Foul water slockens fire,
           And drouth, thir days.

They say, ill ale has been the dead
  O' mony a beardly loun :
Then dinna gape like gleds, wi' greed,
  To sweel hale bickers down.
Gin Lord send mony ane the morn,
  They'll ban fu' sair the time
That e'er they toutit aff the horn,
  Which wambles thro' their wame
           Wi' pain that day.

The Buchan bodies, thro' the beach,
  Their bunch of Findrams cry ;
And skirl out bauld, in Norlan speech,
  " Guid speldins ;—fa will buy ?"
And, by my saul, they're nae wrang gear
  To gust a stirrah's mou ;
Weel staw'd wi' them, he'll never spier
  The price o' being fu'
           Wi' drink that day.

Now wylie wights at rowly-powl,
    And flingin o' the dice,
Here brak the banes o' mony a soul
    Wi' fa's upo' the ice.
At first, the gate seems fair and straught;
    Sae they haud fairly till her:
But, wow! in spite o' a their maught,
    They're rookit o' their siller,
                And gowd, thir days.

Around, whare'er ye fling your een,
    The haiks, like wind, are scourin:
Some chaises honest fock contain;
    And some hae mony a whore in.
Wi' rose and lily, red and white,
    They gie themsels sic fit airs;
Like Dian, they will seem perfite;
    But it's nae gowd that glitters
                Wi' them thir days.

The Lion here, wi' open paw,
    May cleek in mony hunder,
Wha geck at Scotland and her law,
    His wylie talons under:
For, ken, tho' Jamie's laws are auld,
    (Thanks to the wise recorder!)
His Lion yet roars loud and bauld,
    To haud the Whigs in order,
                Sae prime this day.

To town-guard drum of clangour clear,
  Baith men and steeds are raingit:
Some liveries red or yellow wear;
  And some are tartan spraingit.
And now the red,—the blue e'en now,—
  Bids fairest for the market;
But, ere the sport be done, I trow,
  Their skins are gayly yarkit,
          And peel'd, thir days.

Siclike in Robinhood debates,
  Whan twa chiels hae a pingle:
E'en now, some coulie gets his aits,
  And dirt wi' words they mingle;
Till up loups he, wi' diction fu',
  There's lang and dreech contestin;
For now they're near the point in view;—
  Now, ten miles frae the question
          In hand that night.

The races owre, they hale the dools
  Wi' drink o' a kinkind;
Great feck gae hirpling hame, like fools,
  The cripple lead the blind.
May ne'er the canker o' the drink
  Mak our bauld spirits thrawart,
'Case we get wherewitha' to wink
  Wi' een as blue's a blawart,
          Wi' straiks thir days!

THE FARMER'S INGLE.

Et multo in primis hilarans convivia Baccho,
Ante focum, si frigus erit.

VIRG. BUC.

WHAN gloamin grey out-owre the welkin keeks;
　Whan Batie ca's his owsen to the byre;
Whan Thrasher John, sair dung, his barn-door
　　steeks,
　And lusty lasses at the dightin tire;
What bangs fu' leal the e'enings coming cauld,
　And gars snaw-tappit Winter freeze in vain;
Gars dowie mortals look baith blithe and bauld,
　Nor fley'd wi' a' the poortith o' the plain;
　Begin, my Muse! and chant in hamely strain.

Frae the big stack, weel winnow't on the hill,
　Wi' divots theekit frae the weet and drift;
Sods, peats, and heathery trufs the chimley fill,
　And gar their thickening smeek salute the lift.

The gudeman, new come hame, is blithe to find,
   Whan he out-owre the hallan flings his een,
That ilka turn is handled to his mind ;
    That a' his housie looks sae cosh and clean ;
    For cleanly house loes he, tho' e'er sae mean.

Weel kens the gudewife, that the pleughs re-
      quire
   A heartsome meltith, and refreshin synd
O' nappy liquor, owre a bleezin fire :
    Sair wark and poortith downa weel be join'd.
Wi' butter'd bannocks now the girdle reeks ;
   I' the far nook the bowie briskly reams ;
The readied kail stands by the chimley cheeks,
    And haud the riggin het wi' welcome streams,
    Whilk than the daintiest kitchen nicer seems.

Frae this, lat gentler gabs a lesson lear :
   Wad they to labouring lend an eident hand,
They'd rax fell strang upo' the simplest fare,
   Nor find their stamacks ever at a stand.
Fu' hale and healthy wad they pass the day ;
   At night, in calmest slumbers dose fu' sound ;
Nor doctor need their weary life to spae,
    Nor drogs their noddle and their sense con-
      found,
    Till death slip sleely on, and gie the hind-
      most wound.

On sicken food has mony a doughty deed
  By Caledonia's ancestors been done ;
By this did mony a wight fu' weirlike bleed
  In brulzies frae the dawn to set o' sun.
'Twas this that braced their gardies stiff and
      strang ;
  That bent the deadly yew in ancient days ;
Laid Denmark's daring sons on yird alang ;
  Gar'd Scottish thristles bang the Roman bays ;
  For near our crest their heads they doughtna
      raise.

The couthy cracks begin whan supper's owre ;
  The cheering bicker gars them glibly gash
O' Simmer's showery blinks, and Winter sour,
  Whase floods did erst their mailin's produce
      hash.
'Bout kirk and market eke their tales gae on ;
  How Jock woo'd Jenny here to be his bride ;
And there, how Marion, for a bastard son,
  Upo' the cutty-stool was forced to ride ;
  The waefu' scauld o' our Mess John to bide.

The fient a cheep's amang the bairnies now ;
  For a' their anger's wi' their hunger gane :
Ay maun the childer, wi' a fastin mou',
  Grumble and greet, and mak an unco mane.

In rangles round, before the ingle's lowe,
    Frae Gudame's mouth auld-warld tales they
      hear,
O' warlocks loupin round the wirrikow :
    O' ghaists that win in glen and kirkyard
      drear,
    Whilk touzles a' their tap, and gars them
      shake wi' fear!

For weel she trows that fiends and fairies be
    Sent frae the deil to fleetch us to our ill;
That kye hae tint their milk wi' evil ee ;
    And corn been scowder'd on the glowin kill.
O mock na this, my friends ! but rather mourn,
    Ye in life's brawest spring wi' reason clear ;
Wi' eild our idle fancies a' return,
    And dim our dolefu' days wi' bairnly fear ;
    The mind's ay cradled whan the grave is near.

Yet thrift, industrious, bides her latest days,
    Tho' age her sair-dow'd front wi' runcles wave;
Yet frae the russet lap the spindle plays ;
    Her e'enin stent reels she as weel's the lave.
On some feast-day, the wee things, buskit braw,
    Shall heeze her heart up wi' a silent joy,
Fu' cadgie that her head was up, and saw
    Her ain spun cleedin on a darlin oy ;
    Careless tho' death shou'd mak the feast her
      foy.

In its auld lerroch yet the deas remains,
  Whare the gudeman aft streeks him at his
    ease ;
A warm and canny lean for weary banes
  O' lab'rers doil'd upon the wintry leas.
Round him will baudrins and the collie come,
  To wag their tail, and cast a thankfu' ee
To him wha kindly flings them mony a crum
  O' kebbuck whang'd, and dainty fadge to prie;
  This a' the boon they crave, and a' the fee.

Frae him the lads their mornin counsel tak ;
  What stacks he wants to thrash ; what rigs
    to till ;
How big a birn maun lie on Bassie's back,
  For meal and mu'ter to the thirlin mill.
Neist, the gudewife her hirelin damsels bids
  Glowr thro' the byre, and see the hawkies
    bound ;
Tak tent, 'case Crummy tak her wonted tids,
  And ca' the laiglen's treasure on the ground,
  Whilk spills a kebbuck nice, or yellow pound.

Then a' the house for sleep begin to grien,
  Their joints to slack frae industry a-while ;
The leaden god fa's heavy on their een,
  And hafflins steeks them frae their daily toil ;

The cruizie too can only blink and bleer ;
　　The restit ingle's done the maist it dow ;
Tacksman and cotter eke to bed maun steer,
　　Upo' the cod to clear their drumly pow,
　　Till wauken'd by the dawnin's ruddy glow.

Peace to the husbandman and a' his tribe,
　　Whase care fells a' our wants frae year to year !
Lang may his sock and cou'ter turn the glybe,
　　And bauks o' corn bend down wi' laded ear !
May Scotia's simmers ay look gay and green ;
　　Her yellow har'sts frae scowry blasts decreed !
May a' her tenants sit fu' snug and bien,
　　Frae the hard grip o' ails, and poortith freed ;
　　And a lang lasting train o' peacefu' hours suc-
　　　ceed !

THE ELECTION.

Nunc est bibendum, et bendere BICKERUM magnum;
Cavete TOWN-GUARDUM, D——L G—DD—M atque
C—PB—M.

REJOICE, ye Burghers! ane and a';
   Lang look't-for's come at last:
Sair were your backs held to the wa',
   Wi' poortith and wi' fast.
Now ye may clap your wings and craw,
   And gayly busk ilk feather,
For deacon cocks hae pass'd a law,
   To rax and weet your leather
               Wi' drink thir days.

Haste, Epps! quo' John, and bring my giz;
   Tak tent ye dinna't spulzie:
Last night the barber gae't a friz,
   And straikit it wi' ulzie.

Hae done your parritch, lassie Liz !
 Gie me my sark and gravat ;
I'se be as braw's the deacon is,
 Whan he taks affidavit
    O' faith the day.

" Whare's Johnny gaun (cries neebour Bess),
 " That he's sae gayly bodin,
" Wi' new-kam'd wig, weel syndet face,
 " Silk hose, for hamely hodin ?"
' Our Johnny's nae sma drink, you'll guess ;
 ' He's trig as ony muircock,
' And forth to mak a deacon, lass ;
 ' He downa speak to poor fouk
    ' Like us the day.'

The coat, ben-by i' the kist-nook,
 That's been this towmonth swarmin,
Is brought aince mair thereout to look,
 To fleg awa the vermin.
Menzies o' moths and flaes are shook,
 And i' the floor they howder,
Till, in a birn, beneath the crook,
 They're singit wi' a scowder
    To death that day.

The canty cobler quats his sta',
 His roset and his lingans ;

His buik has dree'd a sair, sair fa',
    Frae meals o' bread and ingans.
Now he's a pow o' wit and law,
    And taunts at soals and heels ;
To Walker's he can rin awa,
    There whang his creams and jeels
                Wi' life that day.

The lads, in order tak their seat ;
    (The deil may claw the clungest !)
They stech and connach sae the meat,
    Their teeth mak mair than tongue haste.
Their claes sae cleanly tight and feat,
    And eke their craw-black beavers,
Like masters mows hae fund the gate
    To tassels teugh wi' slavers
                Fu' lang that day.

The dinner done,—for brandy strang
    They cry, to weet their thrapple ;
To gar the stamack bide the bang,
    Nor wi' its ladin graple.
The grace is said ;—it's nae owre lang :—
    The claret reams in bells ;—
Quo' Deacon, " Let the toast round gang :
" Come, Here's our Noble Sels
                " Weel met the day !"

Weels me o' drink, quo cooper Will,
　My barrel has been geyz'd ay,
And has na gotten sic a fill,
　Sin fou on Hansel-Teysday:
But maks na; now it's got a sweel;
　Ae gird I shanna cast, lad!
Or, else, I wish the horned deil
　May Will wi' kittle cast dad
　　　　　To hell the day!

The magistrates fu' wylie are;
　Their lamps are gayly blinkin';
But they might as lieve burn elsewhere,
　Whan fouk's blind-fou' wi drinkin.
Our Deacon wadna ca' a chair;
　The foul ane durst him na-say!
He took shanks-naig; but, fient may care!
　He arslins kiss'd the cawsey
　　　　　Wi' bir that night.

Weel loes me o' you, souter Jock!
　For tricks ye buit be tryin':
Whan grapin for his ain bed-stock,
　He fa's whare Will's wife's lyin,
Will, comin hame wi' ither fouk,
　He saw Jock there before him;
Wi' maister laiglen, like a brock,
　He did wi' stink maist smore him,
　　　　　Fu' strang that night.

Then wi' a souple leathern whang
   He gart them fidge and girn ay :—
" Faith, chiel ! ye's no for naething gang,
   " Gin ye maun reel my pirny."
Syne, wi' a muckle elshin lang
   He brogit Maggie's hurdies ;
And 'cause he thought her i' the wrang,
   There pass'd nae bonny wordies
              'Tween them that night.

Now, had some laird his lady fand
   In sic unseemly courses,
It might hae lows'd the haly band,
   Wi' law-suits and divorces :
But the niest day, they a' shook hands,
   And ilka crack did sowder,
While Meg for drink her apron pawns,
   For a' the gudeman cow'd her
              Whan fu' last night.

Glowr round the cawsey, up and down,
   What mobbing and what plotting !
Here politicians bribe a lown
   Against his saul for voting.
The gowd that inlakes half a crown
   Thir blades lug out to try them,
They pouch the gowd, nor fash the town
   For weights and scales to weigh them
             Exact that day.

Then Deacons at the counsel stent
    To get themsel's presentit :
For towmonths twa their saul is lent,
    For the town's gude indentit :
Lang's their debating thereanent,
    About protests they're bauthrin ;
While Sandy Fife, to mak content,
    On bells plays, " Clout the Caudron,"
                To them that day.

Ye lowns that troke in doctor's stuff,
    You'll now hae unco slaisters ;
Whan windy blaws their stamacks puff,
    They'll need baith pills and plaisters :
For tho' e'en-now they look right bluff,
    Sic drinks, ere hillocks meet,
Will hap some deacons in a truf,
    Inrow'd i' the lang leet
                O' death yon night.

TO THE TRON-KIRK BELL.

Wanwordy, crazy, dinsome thing,
As e'er was fram'd to jow or ring,
What gar'd them sic in steeple hing
      They ken themsel',
But weel wat I they cou'dna bring
      Waur sounds frae hell.

What deil are ye? that I shou'd bann,
Your neither kin to pat nor pan,
Nor ulzie pig, nor maister cann,
      But weel may gie
Mair pleasure to the ear o' man
      Than stroke o' thee.

Fleece merchants may look bauld, I trow,
Sin' a' Auld Reikie's childer now
Maun stap their lugs wi' teats o' woo,
      Thy sound to bang,
And keep it frae gaun thro' and thro'
      Wi' jarrin twang.

Your noisy tongue, there's nae abidin't,
Like scaulding wife's, there is nae guidin't:
Whan I'm 'bout ony bis'ness eident,
    Its sair to thole:
To deave me, then, ye tak a pride in't
     Wi' senseless knoll.

O! were I provost o' the town,
I swear by a' the pow'rs aboon!
I'd bring ye wi' a reesle down;
     Nor shou'd you think
(Sae sair I'd crack and clour your crown)
    Again to clink.

For whan I've toom'd the meikle cap,
And fain wad fa' owre in a nap,
Troth I cou'd dose as soun's a tap,
     Wer't na for thee,
That gies the tither weary chap
    To waken me.

I dreamt ae night I saw Auld Nick;
Quo' he, " This bell o' mine's a trick,
" A wylie piece o' politic,
     " A cunnin snare
" To trap fouk in a cloven stick,
     " Ere they're aware.

" As lang's my dautit bell hings there,
" A' body at the kirk will skair ;
" Quo' they, gif he that preaches there
    " Like it can wound,
" We dinna care a single hair
    " For joyfu' sound."

If magistrates wi' me wad gree,
For ay tongue-tackit shou'd you be ;
Nor fleg wi' anti-melody
    Sic honest fouk,
Whase lugs were never made to dree
    Thy dolefu' shock.

But, far frae thee the bailies dwell,
Or they wad scunner at thy knell ;
Gie the Foul Thief his riven bell,
    And then, I trow,
The by-word hauds, " The deil himsel
    " Has got his due."

MUTUAL COMPLAINT OF

PLAINSTANES AND CAUSEY,

In their Mother Tongue.

Sin' Merlin laid Auld Reikie's causey,
And made her o' his wark right saucy,
The spacious street and gude plainstanes
Were never kend to crack but anes,
Which happen'd on the hinder night,
Whan Fraser's * ulzie tint its light;
O' Highland sentries nane were waukin,
To hear their cronies glibly taukin;
For them this wonder might hae rotten,
And, like night robb'ry, been forgotten,
Hadna a cadie, wi' his lanthorn,
Been gleg enough to hear them bant'rin,
Wha cam to me neist mornin early,
To gie me tidings o' this ferly.

* The Contractor for the lamps.

Ye tauntin lowns, trow this nae joke,
For anes the ass o' Balaam spoke,
Better than lawyers do, forsooth,
For it spak naething but the truth !
Whether they follow its example,
You'll ken best whan you hear the sample.

PLAINSTANES.

My friend, thir hunder years and mair
We've been forfoughen late and ear',
In sunshine, and in weety weather,
Our thrawart lot we bure thegither.
I never growl'd, but was content
Whan ilk ane had an equal stent,
But now to flyte I'se een be bauld,
When I'm wi' sic a grievance thrall'd :
How haps it, say, that mealy bakers,
Hair-kaimers, creeshy gizy-makers,
Shou'd a' get leave to waste their powders
Upo' my beaux and ladies shoulders ?
My travellers are fley'd to deid
Wi' creels wanchancy, heap'd wi' bread,
Frae whilk hing down uncanny nicksticks,
That aften gie the maidens sic licks,
As mak them blithe to skreen their faces
Wi' hats and muckle maun bon-graces,
And cheat the lads that fain wad see
The glances o' a pauky ee,

Or gie their loves a wylie wink,
That erst might lend their hearts a clink !
Speak, was I made to dree the ladin
O' Gallic chairmens' heavy treadin,
Wha in my tender buke bore holes
Wi' waefu' tackets i' the soals
O' broggs, whilk on my body tramp,
And wound like death at ilka clamp ?

CAWSEY.

Weel crackit, friend !—It aft hauds true,
'Bout naething fouk mak maist ado.
Weel ken ye, tho' ye doughtna tell,
I pay the sairest kain mysel,
Owre me, ilk day, big waggons rumble,
And a' my fabric birze and jumble.
Owre me the muckle horses gallop,
Eneugh to rug my very saul up ;
And coachmen never trow they're sinnin',
While down the street their wheels are spinnin'.
Like thee, do I not bide the brunt
O' Highland chairmens' heavy dunt ?
Yet I hae never thought o' breathing
Complaint, or makin din for naething.

PLAINSTANES.

Haud sae, and let me get a word in ;
Your back's best fitted for the burden :

And I can eithly tell you why,
Ye're doughtier by far than I :
For whinstanes houkit frae the craigs,
May thole the prancin feet o' naigs,
Nor ever fear uncanny hotches
Frae clumsy carts or hackney coaches ;
While I, a weak and feckless creature,
Am moulded by a safter nature.
Wi' mason's chissel dighted neat,
To gar me look baith clean and feat,
I scarce can bear a sairer thump
Than comes frae soal o' shoe or pump.
I grant, indeed, that now and then,
Yield to a paten's pith I maun :
But patens, tho' they're aften plenty,
Are ay laid down wi' feet fu' tenty ;
And strokes frae ladies, tho' they're teazin,
I freely maun avow are pleasin.

    For what use was I made, I wonder ?
It was na tamely to chap under
The weight o' ilka codroch chiel,
That does my skin to targets peel.
But gin I guess aright, my trade is
To fend frae skaith the bonny ladies ;
To keep the bairnies free frae harms
Whan airin i' their nurses' arms ;
To be a safe and canny bield
For grown youth or droopin eild.

Tak then frae me the heavy load
O' burden-bearers heavy shod;
Or, by my troth, the gude auld town sall
Hae this affair before the Council.

CAWSEY.

I dinna care a single jot;
Tho' summon'd by a shelly-coat;
Sae lealy I'll propone defences,
As get ye flung for my expences.
Your libel I'll impugn *verbatim*,
And hae a *magnum damnum datum:*
For, tho' frae Arthur's Seat I sprang,
And am in constitution strang,
Wad it na fret the hardest stane
Beneath the Luckenbooths to grane?
Tho' magistrates the Cross discard,
It maks na, whan they leave the Guard,—
A lumbersome and stinkin biggin,
That rides the sairest on my riggin.
Poor me o'er meikle do ye blame,
For tradesmen trampin on your wame;
Yet a' your advocates, and braw fouk,
Come still to me 'twixt ane and twa o'clock,
And never yet were kent to range
At Charlie's Statue or Exchange.
Then, tak your beax and macaronies;
Gie me trades' fouk, and country Johnnies;

The deil's in't gin ye dinna sign
Your sentiments conjunct wi' mine.

PLAINSTANES.

Gin we twa cou'd be as auldfarrant,
As gar the Council gie a warrant,
Ilk loun rebellious to tak,
Wha walks not i' the proper track,
And o' three shillins Scottish suck him ;
Or in the water-hole sair douk him ;
This might assist the poor's collection,
And gie baith parties satisfaction.

CAWSEY.

But first, I think, it will be good,
To bring it to the Robinhood *,
Whare we sall hae the question stated,
And keen and crabbitly debated,—
Whether the provost and the bailies,
For the town's gude whase daily toil is,
Shou'd listen to our joint petitions,
And see obtemper'd the conditions.

PLAINSTANES.

Content am I.—But east the gate is
The Sun, wha taks his leave o' Thetis,

* A debating society ; afterwards called the Pantheon.

And comes to wauken honest fouk,
That gang to wark at sax o'clock.
It sets us to be dumb a while,
And let our words gie place to toil.

=====

A DRINK ECLOGUE.

LANDLADY, BRANDY, AND WHISKY.

On auld worm-eaten skelf, in cellar dunk,
Whare hearty benders seynd their drouthy
    trunk,
Twa chappin bottles, bang'd wi' liquor fu,—
Brandy the tane,—the tither Whisky blue,—
Grew canker'd ; for the twa were het within,
And het-skinn'd fouk to flytin soon begin.
The Frenchman fizz'd, and first wad foot the
    field,
While paughty Scotsman scorn'd to beenge or
    yield.

BRANDY.

Black be your fa', ye cotter loun mislear'd!
Blawn by the Porters, Chairmen, City Guard:
Hae ye nae breedin, that you cock your nose
Against my sweetly-gusted cordial dose?
I've been near pawky courts, and, aften there,
Hae ca'd hysterics frae the dowie fair;
And courtiers aft gaed greenin for my smack,
To gar them bauldly glowr, and gashly crack.
The priest, to bang mishanters black, and cares,
Has sought me in his closet for his prayers.
What tid then taks the fates, that they can thole
Thrawart to fix me i' this weary hole,
Sair fash'd wi' din, wi' darkness, and wi' stinks,
Whare cheery day-light thro' the mirk ne'er
    blinks?

WHISKY.

But ye maun be content, and maunna rue,
Tho' erst ye've bizz'd in bonny madam's mou.
Wi' thoughts like thae, your heart may sairly
    dunt,
The warld's now chang'd; it's nae like use and
    wont:
For here, wae's me! there's nouther lord nor
    laird
Comes to get heartscad frae their stamack
    skair'd.

Nae mair your courtier louns will shaw their face;
For they glowr eery at a friend's disgrace.
But heese your heart up :—Whan at court you
  hear
The patriot's thrapple wat wi' reamin beer;
Whan chairman, weary wi' his daily gain,
Cah seynd his whistle wi' the clear Champaign;
Be hopefu', for the time will soon row round,
Whan you'll nae langer dwall beneath the ground.

BRANDY.

Wanwordy gowk ! did I sae aften shine
Wi' gowden glister thro' the crystal fine,
To thole your taunts, that seenil hae been seen
Awa frae luggie, quegh, or truncher treein;
Gif honour wad but let, a challenge shou'd
Twine ye o' Highland tongue and Highland
  blude;
Wi' cards like thee I scorn to file my thumb;
For gentle spirits gentle breedin doom.

WHISKY.

Truly, I think it right you get your alms,
Your high heart humbled amang common
  drams :
Braw days for you, whan fools, newfangle fain,
Like ither countries better than their ain;
For there ye never saw sic chancy days,
Sic balls, assemblies, operas, or plays;

Hame-o'er langsyne you hae been blithe to pack
Your a' upon a sarkless soldier's back ;
For you thir lads, as weel-lear'd trav'llers tell,
Had sell'd their sarks, gin sarks they had to sell.

 But Worth gets poortith an' black burnin
   shame,
To draunt and drivel out a life at hame.
Alake ! the byword's owr weel kent throughout,
" Prophets at hame are held in nae repute ;"
Sae fair'st wi' me, tho' I can heat the skin,
And set the saul upo' a merry pin,
Yet I am hameil ; there's the sour mischance !
I'm na frae Turkey, Italy, or France ;
For now our gentles gabs are grown sae nice,
At thee they tout, and never speer my price :
Witness—for thee they height their tenants rent,
And fill their lands wi' poortith, discontent ;
Gar them o'er seas for cheaper mailins hunt,
And leave their ain as bare's the Cairney mount.

BRANDY.

Tho' lairds tak toothfu's o' my warming sap,
This dwines not tenants' gear, nor cows their
   crap ;
For love to you there's mony a tenant gaes
Bare-ars'd and barefoot o'er the highland braes :

For you nae mair the thrifty gudewife sees
Her lasses kirn, or birze the dainty cheese;
Crummie nae mair for Jenny's hand will crune,
Wi' milkness dreeping frae her teats adown :
For you owre ear' the ox his fate partakes,
And fa's a victim to the bluidy ax.

WHISKY.

Wha is't that gars the greedy bankers prieve
The maiden's tocher, but the maiden's leave :
By you whan spulzied o' her charming pose,
She tholes in turn the taunt o' cauldrife joes.
Wi' skelps like this fouk sit but seenil down
To wether-gammon, or howtowdy brown ;
Sair dung wi' dule, and fley'd for coming debt,
They gar their mou'-bits wi' their incomes mett,
Content enough gif they hae wherewithal
Scrimply to tack their body and their saul.

BRANDY.

Frae some poor poet, o'er as poor a pot,
Ye've lear'd to crack sae crouse, ye haveril Scot,
Or burgher politician, that embrues
His tongue in thee, and reads the claiking news ;
But waes heart for you ! that for ay maun dwell
In poet's garret, or in chairman's cell,
While I shall yet on bein-clad tables stand,
Boudin wi' a' the daintiths o' the land.

WHISKY.

Troth I hae been ere now the poet's flame,
And heez'd his sangs to mony blithesome theme.
Wha was't gar'd ALLIE's chaunter chirm fu'
    clear,
Life to the saul, and music to the ear?
Nae stream but kens, and can repeat the lay,
To shepherds streekit on the simmer-brae,
Wha to their whistle wi' the lav'rock bang,
To wauken flocks the rural fields amang.

BRANDY.

But here's the browster-wife, and she can tell
Wha's won the day, and wha shou'd bear the
    bell :
Hae done your din, an' let her judgment join
In final verdict 'twixt your plea and mine.

LANDLADY.

In days o' yore, I cou'd my living prize,
Nor fash'd wi' dolefu' gaugers or excise ;
But now-a-days we're blithe to lear the thrift
Our heads 'boon licence and excise to lift ;
Inlakes o' Brandy we can soon supply
By Whisky tinctur'd wi' the saffron's dye.

Will you your breeding threep, ye mongrel
    loun !
Frae hame-bred liquor dyed to colour brown?

So flunky braw, whan drest in maister's claise,
Struts to Auld Reikie's cross on sunny days,
Till some auld comrade, ablins out o' place,
Near the vain upstart shaws his meagre face;
Bumbaz'd he loups frae sight, and jooks his ken,
Fley'd to be seen amang the tassel'd train.

LINES,

To the PRINCIPAL *and* PROFESSORS *of the University of St Andrews, on their superb Treat to* DR SAMUEL JOHNSON.

ST ANDREW's town may look right gawsy;
Nae grass will grow upo' her cawsey,
Nor wa'-flowers o' a yellow dye,
Glowr dowie owre her ruins high,
Sin' Samy's head, weel pang'd wi' lear,
Has seen the *Alma Mater* there.
Regents! my winsome billy boys!
'Bout him you've made an unco noise;

Nae doubt, for him your bells wad clink,
To find him upon Eden's brink;
And a' things nicely set in order,
Wad keep him on the Fifan border.
I'se warrant, now, frae France and Spain
Baith cooks and scullions mony ane,
Wad gar the pats and kettles tingle
Around the college kitchen ingle,
To fleg frae a' your craigs the roup,
Wi' reekin het and crieshy soup:
And snails and puddocks mony hunder
Wad beekin lie the hearthstane under;
Wi' roast and boil'd, and a' kinkind,
To heat the body, cool the mind.

But hear, my lads! gin I'd been there,
How I'd hae trimm'd the bill o' fare!
For ne'er sic surly wight as he
Had met wi' sic respect frae me.
Mind ye what Sam, the lyin loun!
Has in his Dictionar laid down?
That aits, in England, are a feast
To cow and horse, and sicken beast;
While, in Scots ground, this growth was com-
    mon
To gust the gab o' man and woman.
Tak tent, ye Regents! then, and hear
My list o' gudely hameil gear;

R r

Sic as hae aften rax'd the wyme
O' blyther fallows mony time;
Mair hardy, souple, steeve, and swank,
Than ever stood on Samy's shank.

Imprimis, then, a haggis fat,
Weel tottled in a seything pat,
Wi' spice and ingans weel ca'd thro',
Had help'd to gust the stirrah's mou,
And plac'd itsel in truncher clean
Before the gilpy's glowrin een.

Secundo, then, a gude sheep's head,
Whase hide was singit, never flea'd,
And four black trotters clad wi' girsle,
Bedown his throat had learn'd to hirsle.
What think ye, niest, o' gude fat brose,
To clag his ribs, a dainty dose?
And white and bluidy puddings routh,
To gar the Doctor skirl, " O Drouth!"
Whan he cou'd never houp to merit
A cordial glass o' reamin claret,
But thraw his nose, and birze, and pegh,
Owre the contents o' sma' ale quegh.
Then, let his wisdom girn and snarl
O'er a weel-tostit girdle farl,
And learn, that, maugre o' his wyme,
Ill bairns are ay best heard at hame.

Drummond, lang syne, o' Hawthornden,
The wyliest and best o' men,
Has gien you dishes ane or mae,
That wad hae gar'd his grinders play,
Not to " Roast Beef*," old England's life !
But to the auld " East Nook o' Fife*,"
Where Craillian crafts cou'd weel hae gien
Skate-rumples to hae clear'd his een ;
Then, niest, whan Samy's heart was faintin,
He'd lang'd for skate to mak him wanton.

Ah, willawins for Scotland now !
Whan she maun stap ilk birky's mou
Wi' eistacks, grown as 'twere in pet
In foreign land, or greenhouse het,
Whan cog o' brose, and cutty spoon,
Is a' your cottar childers' boon,
Wha thro' the week, till Sunday's speal,
Toil for pease-clods and gude lang kail.

Devall then, Sirs, and never send
For daintiths to regale a friend ;
Or, like a torch at baith ends burnin,
Your house will soon grow mirk and mournin !

* Alluding to two tunes under these titles.

316

What's this I hear some cynic say*?—
Robin, ye loun! it's nae fair play;
Is there nae ither subject rife
To clap your thumb upon but Fife?
Gie owre, young man! you'll meet your cornin,
Than caption waur, or charge o' hornin;
Some canker'd, surly, sour-mou'd carlin,
Bred near the abbey o' Dumfarline,
Your shoulders yet may gie a lounder,
And be o' verse the mal-confounder.

Come on, ye blades! but ere ye tulzie,
Or hack our flesh wi' sword or gullie,
Ne'er shaw your teeth, nor look like stink,
Nor owre an empty bicker blink:
What weets the wizen and the wyme,
Will mend your prose, and heal my rhyme.

* The Poet alludes to a gentleman in Dunfermline, who
sent him a challenge, being highly offended at the conclud-
ing reflection in the " Expedition to Fife."

ELEGY ON JOHN HOGG,

Porter to the University of St Andrew's.

DEATH ! what's ado ? the deil be licket,
Or wi' your stang you ne'er had pricket,
Or our auld *Alma Mater* tricket,
      O' poor John Hogg,
And trail'd him ben thro' your mark wicket,
      As dead's a log.

Now ilka glaikit scholar loun
May dander wae wi' duddy gown ;
Kate Kennedy* to dowie crune
      May mourn and clink,
And steeples o' Saunt Andrew's Town
      To yird may sink.

* A bell in the college steeple.

Sin' Pauly Tam*, wi' canker'd snout,
First held the students in about,
To wear their claes as black as soot,
    They ne'er had reason,
Till Death John's haffit gae a clout,
    Sae out o' season.

Whan Regents met at common schools,
He taught auld Tam to hale the dools,
And eident to row right the bowls,
    Like ony emmack;
He kept us a' within the rules
    Strict academic.

Heh! wha will tell the students now
To meet the Pauly cheek for chow,
Whan he, like frightsome wirrikow,
    Had wont to rail,
And set our stamacks in a low,
    Or we turn'd tail?

Ah, Johnny! aften did I grumble
Frae cozy bed fu' ear' to tumble,
Whan art and part I'd been in some ill,
    Troth, I was swear:
His words they brodit like a wumill,
    Frae ear to ear.

* A name given by the students to one of the members of the University.

Whan I had been fu' laith to rise,
John then begude to moralize :
" The tither nap, the sluggard cries,
   " And turns him round :
" Sae spak auld Solomon the wise,
   " Divine profound !"

Nae dominie, or wise Mess John,
Was better lear'd in Solomon ;
He cited proverbs, one by one,
   Ilk vice to tame ;
He gar'd ilk sinner sigh and groan,
   And fear hell's flame.

" I hae nae meikle skill, (quo' he),
" In what you ca' philosophy ;
" It tells that baith the earth and sea
   " Rin round about :
" Either the Bible tells a lie,
   " Or ye're a' out.

" It's i' the Psalms o' David writ,
" That this wide warld ne'er shou'd flit,
" But on the waters coshly sit
   " Fu' steeve and lastin :
" And was na he a head o' wit
   " At sic contestin ?"

On e'enings cauld wi' glee we'd trudge
To heat our shins in Johnny's lodge :
The deil ane thought his bum to budge
      Wi' siller on us :
To claw het pints we'd never grudge
      O' *molationis.*

Say, ye red gowns ! that aften, here,
Hae toasted cakes to Katie's beer,
Gin e'er thir days hae had their peer,
      Sae blithe, sae daft ?
You'll ne'er again, in life's career,
      Sit half sae saft.

Wi' haffit locks, sae smooth and sleek,
John look'd like ony ancient Greek :
He was a Naz'rene a' the week,
      And doughtna tell out
A bawbee Scots to scrape his cheek,
      Till Sunday fell out.

For John ay lo'ed to turn the pence ;
Thought poortith was a great offence :
" What recks, tho' ye ken mood and tense ?
      " A hungry wyme
" For gowd wad wi' them baith dispense,
      " At ony time.

" Ye ken what ills maun ay befal
" The chiel that will be prodigal ;
" Whan wasted to the very spaul,
     " He turns his tusk,
" (For want o' comfort to his saul)
     " O' hungry husk."

Ye royit louns ! just do as he'd do :
For mony braw green shaw and meadow
He's left to cheer his dowie widow,
     His winsome Kate,
That to him prov'd a canny she-dow,
     Baith ear' and late.

THE GHAISTS,

A Kirk-Yard Eclogue.

Did you not say, in good Ann's day,
And vow, and did protest, Sir,
That when Hanover should come o'er,
We surely should be blest, Sir ?

AN AULD SANG MADE NEW AGAIN.

WHARE the braid planes in dowie murmurs wave
Their ancient taps out owre the cauld-clad grave,
Whare Geordie Girdwood *, mony a lang-spun
    day,
Houkit for gentlest banes the humblest clay,
Twa sheeted ghaists, sae grizly and sae wan,
'Mang lanely tombs their douff discourse began.

* The late Sexton.

WATSON.

Cauld blaws the nippin North wi' angry seugh,
And showers his hailstanes frae the Castle Cleugh
Owre the Grayfriars, whare, at mirkest hour,
Bogles and spectres wont to tak their tour,
Harlin the pows and shanks to hidden cairns,
Amang the hemlocks wild, and sun-brunt ferns ;
But nane the night, save you and I, hae come
Frae the drear mansions o' the midnight tomb.
Now, whan the dawnin's near, whan cock maun
    craw,
And wi' his angry bougil gar's withdraw,
Ayont the kirk we'll stap, and there tak bield,
While the black hours our nightly freedom yield.

HERIOT.

I'm weel content : but, binna cassen down,
Nor trow the cock will ca' ye hame o'er soon ;
For, tho' the eastern lift betakens day,
Changing her rokelay black for mantle gray,
Nae weirlike bird our knell of parting rings,
Nor sheds the cauler moisture frae his wings.
Nature has chang'd her course ; the birds o' day
Dosin in silence on the bendin spray,
While howlets round the craigs at noontide flee,
And bluidy hawks sit singin on the tree.
Ah, Caledon ! the land I aince held dear ;
Sair mane mak I for thy destruction near :

And thou, Edina ! aince my dear abode,
Whan royal Jamie sway'd the sov'reign rod,
In thae blest days, weel did I think bestow'd
To blaw thy poortith by wi' heaps o' gowd ;
To mak thee sonsy seem wi' mony a gift,
And gar thy stately turrets speel the lift.
In vain did Danish Jones, wi' gimcrack pains,
In Gothic sculpture fret the pliant stanes ;
In vain did he affix my statue here,
Brawly to busk wi' flowers ilk coming year.
My towers are sunk ; my lands are barren now ;
My fame, my honour, like my flowers, maun dow.

WATSON.

Sure, Major Weir, or some sic warlock wight,
Has flung beguilin glamour owre your sight ;
Or else some kittle cantrip thrown, I ween,
Has bound in mirlygoes my ain twa een :
If ever aught frae sense cou'd be believ'd
(And seenil hae my senses been deceiv'd),
'This moment owre the tap o' Adam's tomb,
Fu' easy can I see your chiefest dome.
Nae corbie fleein there, nor croupin craws,
Seem to forspeak the ruin o' thy ha's ;
But a' your towers in wonted order stand,
Steeve as the rocks that hem our native land.

HERIOT.

Think na I vent my well-a-day in vain ;
Kent ye the cause, ye sure wad join my mane.

Black be the day, that e'er to England's ground
Scotland was eikit by the Union's bond!
For mony a menzie o' destructive ills
The country now maun brook frae mortmain
          bills,
That void our test'ments, and can freely gie
Sic will and scoup to the ordain'd trustee,
That he may tir our stateliest riggins bare;
Nor acres, houses, woods, nor fishings spare,
Till he can lend the stoiterin state a lift,
Wi' gowd in gowpins, as a grassum gift;
In lieu o' whilk, we maun be weel content
To tine the capital for *three per cent.;*
A doughty sum indeed; whan, now-a-days,
They raise provisions as the stents they raise;
Yoke hard the poor, and lat the rich chields be
Pamper'd at ease by ithers' industry.

Hale interest for my fund can scantly now
Cleed a' my callants' backs, and stap their mou'.
How maun their wymes wi' sairest hunger slack,
Their duds in targets flaff upon their back,
Whan they are doom'd to keep a lastin Lent,
Starving for England's weel, at *three per cent.!*

WATSON.
Auld Reikie then may bless the gowden times,
Whan honesty and poortith baith are crimes.

She little ken'd, whan you and I endow'd
Our hospitals for back-gaun burghers' gude,
That e'er our siller or our lands shou'd bring
A gude bien livin to a back-gaun king ;
Wha, thanks to Ministry ! is grown sae wise,
He downa chew the bitter cud o' vice :
For gin, frae Castlehill to Netherbow,
Wad honest houses bawdy-houses grow,
The Crown wad never spier.the price o' sin,
Nor hinder younkers to the deil to rin ;
But, gif some mortal grien for pious fame,
And leave the poor man's prayer to sane his
      name,
His gear maun a' be scatter'd by the claws
O' ruthless, ravenous, and harpy laws.
Yet, shou'd I think, although the bill tak place,
The council winna lack sae meikle grace
As lat our heritage at wanworth gang,
Or the succeeding generations wrang
O' braw bein maintenance, and walth o' lear,
Whilk else had drappit to their children's skair;
For mony a deep, and mony a rare engine
Hae sprung frae Heriot's Wark, and sprung
      frae mine.

HERIOT.

I find, my friend ! that ye but little ken,
There's e'en now on the earth a set o' men,

Wha, if they get their private pouches lin'd,
Gie na a winnlestrae for a' mankind.
They'll sell their country, flae their conscience
        bare,
To gar the weigh-bauk turn a single hair.
The Government need only bait the line
Wi' the prevailin flee—the gowden coin!
Then our executors, and wise trustees,
Will sell them fishes in forbidden seas :
Upo' their dwinin country girn in sport ;
Laugh in their sleeve, and get a place at court.

WATSON.

Ere that day come, I'll 'mang our spirits pick
Some ghaist that trokes and conjures wi' Auld
        Nick,
To gar the wind wi' rougher rumbles blaw,
And weightier thuds than ever mortal saw :
Fireflaught and hail, wi' tenfauld fury's fires,
Shall lay yird-laigh Edina's airy spires :
Tweed shall rin rowtin down his banks out
        owre,
Till Scotland's out o' reach o' England's power;
Upo' the briny Borean jaws to float,
And mourn in dowie seughs her dowie lot.

HERIOT.

Yonder's the tomb of wise Mackenzie fam'd,
Whase laws rebellious bigotry reclaim'd ;

Freed the hale land o' covenantin fools,
Wha erst hae fash'd us wi' unnumber'd dools.
Till night, we'll tak the swaird aboon our pows,
And then, whan she her ebon chariot rows,
We'll travel to the vau't wi' stealin stap,
And wauk Mackenzie frae his quiet nap;
Tell him our ails, that he, wi' wonted skill,
May fleg the schemers o' the Mortmain Bill*.

EPISTLE TO

MR ROBERT FERGUSSON.

Is Allan risen frae the dead,
Wha aft has tun'd the aiten reed,
And by the Muses was decreed
       To grace the thistle?
Na:—Fergusson's come in his stead.
       To blaw the whistle.

* This Poem was written about the time a bill was in
agitation for vesting the whole funds of Hospitals, and other
charities throughout the kingdom, in government stock, at
three per cent.

In troth, my callant ! I'm sae fain
To read your sonsy, canty strain ;
You write sic easy style, and plain,
   'And words sae bonny,
Nae Southern loun dare you disdain,
   Or cry, " Fy on ye !"

Whae'er has at auld Reikie been,
And King's birth-days' exploits has seen,
Maun own that ye hae gien a keen
   And true description ;
Nor say, ye've at Parnassus been,
   To form a fiction.

Hale be your heart, ye canty chield !
May ye ne'er want a gude warm bield,
And sic gude cakes as Scotland yield,
   And ilka dainty
That grows or feeds upon her field,
   And whisky plenty.

But ye, perhaps, thirst mair for fame
Than a' the gude things I can name ;
And then, ye will be sair to blame
   My gude intention,
For that ye needna gae frae hame,
   You've sic pretension.

Sae saft and sweet your verses jingle,
And your auld words sae meetly mingle,
'Twill gar baith married fock and single
   To roose your lays:
Whan we forgather round the ingle,
   We'll chaunt your praise.

Whan I again Auld Reikie see,
And can forgather, lad! wi' thee,
Then we, wi' muckle mirth and glee,
   Shall tak a gill,
And o' your cauler oysters we
   Shall eat our fill.

If sic a thing shall you betide,
To Berwick town to tak a ride,
I'se tak ye up Tweed's bonny side,
   Before ye settle,
And shaw you there the fisher's pride,
   A sa'mon kettle.

There lads and lasses do conveen
To feast and dance upo' the green;
And there sic bravery may be seen,
   As will confound ye,
And gar you glowr out baith your een
   At a' around ye.

To see sae mony bosoms bare,
And sic huge puddings i' their hair,
And some o' them wi' naething mair
        Upo' their tete;
Yea, some wi' mutches that might scare
        Craws frae their meat.

I ne'er appear'd before in print,
But, for your sake, wad fain be in't;
E'en that I might my wishes hint,
        That you'd write mair:
For sure your head-piece is a mint
        Whare wit's nae rare.

Sonse fa' me! gif I hadna lure,
I cou'd command ilk Muse as sure,
Than hae a chariot at the door,
        To wait upo' me;
Tho', poet-like, I'm but a poor
        Mid-Lothian Johnny.
                J. S.

Berwick, August 31st, 1773.

ANSWER TO MR J. S.'s EPISTLE.

I TROW, my mettled Louthian lathie !
Auldfarran birky I maun ca' thee ;
For whan in gude black print I saw thee,
   Wi' souple gab,
I skirl'd fu' loud, " Oh wae befa' thee !
   " But thou'rt a daub."

Awa, ye wylie fleetchin fallow !
The rose shall grow like gowan yellow,
Before I turn sae toom and shallow,
   And void o' fusion,
As a' your butter'd words to swallow
   In vain delusion.

Ye mak my Muse a dautit pet ;
But gin she cou'd like Allan's met,
Or couthy cracks and hamely get
   Upo' her carritch,
Eithly wad I be in your debt
   A pint o' parritch.

At times, whan she may lowse her pack,
I'll grant that she can find a knack
To gar auld-warld wordies clack
        In hamespun rhime,
While ilk ane at his billy's back
        Keeps gude Scots time.

But she maun e'en be glad to jook,
And play teet-bo frae nook to nook,
Or blush as gin she had the yook
        Upo' her skin,
Whan Ramsay or whan Pennycuick
        Their lilts begin.

At mornin ear', or late at e'enin,
Gin ye sud hap to come and see ane,
Nor niggard wife, nor greetin wee ane,
        Within my cloister,
Can challenge you and me frae priein
        A cauler oyster.

Heh, lad! it wad be news indeed,
Were I to ride to bonny Tweed,
Wha ne'er laid gammon owre a steed
        Beyont Lusterick ;
And auld shanks-naig wad tire, I dread,
        To pace to Berwick.

You crack weel o' your lasses there;
Their glancin een, and bisket bare;
But, thof this town be smeekit sair,
   I'll wad farden,
Than our's there's nane mare fat and fair,
   Cravin your pardon.

Gin heaven shou'd gie the earth a drink,
And afterhend a sunny blink,
Gin ye were here, I'm sure you'd think
   It worth your notice,
To see them dubs and gutters jink
   Wi' kiltit coaties:

And frae ilk corner o' the nation,
We've lasses eke o' recreation,
Wha at close-mou's tak up their station
   By ten o'clock.—
The Lord deliver frae temptation
   A' honest fouk!

Thir queans are ay upo' the catch
For pursie, pocket-book, or watch,
And can sae glib their leesins hatch,
   That you'll agree,
Ye canna eithly meet their match
   'Tween you and me.

For this gude sample o' your skill,
I'm restin you a pint o' yill,
By an attour a Highland gill
                    O' *Aquavitæ;*
The which to come and sock at will,
                    I here invite ye.

Tho' jillet Fortune scoul and quarrel,
And keep me frae a bien beef barrel,
As lang's I've twopence i' the warl'
                    I'll ay be vockie
To part a fadge or girdle farl
                    Wi' Louthian Jockie.

Fareweel, my cock! lang may you thrive,
Weel happit in a cozy hive;
And that your saul may never dive
                    To Acheron,
I'll wish, as lang's I can subscrive
                    ROB. FERGUSSON.

TO MY AULD BREEKS.

Now gae your wa's.—Tho' aince as gude
As ever happit flesh and blude,
Yet part we maun.—The case sae hard is
Amang the writers and the bardies,
That lang they'll bruik the auld I trow,
Or neebours cry, " Weel bruik the new !"
Still makin tight wi' tither steek ;
The tither hole, the tither eik,
To bang the bir o' Winter's anger,
And haud the hurdies out o' langer.

Siclike some weary wight will fill
His kyte wi' drogs frae doctor's bill,
Thinkin to tack the tither year
To life, and look baith hale and fier ;
Till, at the lang-run, Death dirks in,
To birze his saul ayont his skin.

You needna wag your duds o' clouts,
Nor fa' into your dorty pouts,

To think that erst you've hain'd my tail
Frae wind and weet, frae snaw and hail,
And for reward, whan bauld and hummil,
Frae garret high to dree a tumble.
For you I car'd, as lang's ye dow'd
Be lin'd wi' siller or wi' gowd :
Now to befriend, it wad be folly,
Your raggit hide and pouches holey ;
For wha but kens a poet's placks
Get mony weary flaws and cracks,
And canna thole to hae them tint,
As he sae seenil sees the mint ?
Yet round the warld keek and see,
That ithers fare as ill as thee ;
For weel we loe the chiel we think
Can get us tick, or gie us drink,
Till o' his purse we've seen the bottom,
Then we despise, and hae forgot him.

Yet gratefu' hearts, to mak amends,
Will ay be sorry for their friends,
And I for thee—As mony a time
Wi' you I've speel'd the braes o' rhyme,
Whare for the time the Muse ne'er cares
For siller, or sic guilefu' wares,
Wi' whilk we drumly grow, and crabbit,
Dour, capernoited, thrawin gabbit,
And brither, sister, friend, and fae,
Without remeid o' kindred, slae.

U u

You've seen me round the bickers reel
Wi' heart as hale as temper'd steel,
And face sae open, free, and blithe,
Nor thought that sorrow there cou'd kyth;
But the neist moment this was lost,
Like gowan in December's frost.

Cou'd prick-the-louse but be sae handy
As mak the breeks and claise to stand ay,
Thro' thick and thin wi' you I'd dash on,
Nor mind the folly o' the fashion :
But, heh ! the times' *vicissitudo*
Gars ither breeks decay as you do.
Thae macaronies, braw and windy,
Maun fail—*Sic transit gloria mundi !*

Now speed you to some madam's chaumer,
That but and ben rings dule and clamour,
Ask her, in kindness, if she seeks
In hidling ways to wear the breeks?
Safe you may dwall, tho' mould and motty,
Beneath the veil o' under coatie,
For this mair fauts nor yours can screen
Frae lover's quickest sense, his een.

Or if some bard, in lucky times,
Shou'd profit meikle by his rhymes,
And pace awa, wi' smirky face,
In siller or in gowden lace,

Glowr in his face, like spectre gaunt;
Remind him o' his former want;
To cow his daffin and his pleasure,
And gar him live within the measure.

   So Philip, it is said, who wou'd ring
Owre Macedon, a just and gude king,
Fearing that power might plume his feather,
And bid him stretch beyond the tether,
Ilk mornin to his lug wad ca'
A tiny servant o' his ha',
To tell him to improve his span;
For Philip was, like him, a Man.

AULD REIKIE.

Auld Reikie! wale o' ilka town
That Scotland kens beneath the moon;
Whare couthy chields at e'ening meet
Their bizzin craigs and mou's to weet;
And blithely gar auld Care gae by
Wi' blinkın and wi' bleerin eye.

Owre lang frae thee the Muse has been
Sae frisky on the Simmer's green,
Whan flowers and gowans wont to glent
In bonny blinks upo' the bent :
But now the leaves o' yellow dye,
Peel'd frae the branches quickly fly ;
And now frae nouther bush nor brier
The spreckled mavis greets your ear ;
Nor bonny blackbird skims and roves
To seek his love in yonder groves.
Then, Reikie, welcome ! thou canst charm,
Unfleggit by the year's alarm.
Not Boreas, that sae snelly blows,
Dare here pap in his angry nose,
Thanks to our dads, whase biggin stands
A shelter to surrounding lands!

Now Morn, with bonny purple smiles,
Kisses the air-cock o' Saunt Giles ;
Rakin their een, the servant lasses
Early begin their lies and clashes.
Ilk tells her friend of saddest distress,
That still she bruiks frae scoulin' mistress ;
And wi' her joe in turnpike stair,
She'd rather snuff the stinkin air,
As be subjected to her tongue,
Whan justly censur'd i' the wrong.

On stair, wi' tub or pat in hand,
The barefoot housemaids loe to stand,
That antrin fock may ken how snell
Auld Reikie will at mornin smell :
Then, with an inundation big as
The burn that 'neath the Nor' Loch brig is,
They kindly shower Edina's roses,
To quicken and regale our noses.
Now some for this, wi' Satire's leese,
Hae gien auld Edinbrough a creesh :
But, without scourin nought is sweet ;
The mornin smells that hail our street,
Prepare, and gently lead the way
To Simmer canty, braw, and gay.
Edina's sons mair eithly share
Her spices and her dainties rare,
Than he that's never yet been call'd
Aff frae his plaidie or his fauld.

Now stairhead critics, senseless fools !
Censure their aim, and pride their rules,
In Luckenbooths, wi' glowrin eye,
Their neebours sma'est faults descry.
If ony loun shou'd dander there,
O' awkward gait   d foreign air,
They trace his steps, till they can tell
His pedigree as weel's himsel.

Whan Phœbus blinks wi' warmer ray,
And schools at noon-day get the play,
Then bus'ness, weighty bus'ness, comes;
The trader glowrs; he doubts, he hums.
The lawyers eke to cross repair,
Their wigs to shaw, and toss an air;
While busy agent closely plies,
And a' his kittle cases tries.

Now night, that's cunzied chief for fun,
Is wi' her usual rites begun;
Thro' ilka gate the torches blaze,
And globes send out their blinkin rays.
The usefu' cadie plies in street,
To bide the profits o' his feet;
For, by thir lads Auld Reikie's fouk
Ken but a sample o' the stock
O' thieves, that nightly wad oppress,
And mak baith goods and gear the less.
Near him the lazy chairman stands,
And wats na how to turn his hands,
Till some daft birky, rantin fou,
Has matters somewhere else to do;
The chairman willing gies his light
To deeds o' darkness and o' night.

It's never saxpence for a lift
That gars thir lads wi' fu'ness rift;

For they wi' better gear are paid,
And whores and culls support their trade.

Near some lamp-post, wi' dowie face,
Wi' heavy een, and sour grimace,
Stands she, that beauty lang had kend ;
Whoredom her trade, and vice her end.
But, see whare now she wins her bread
By that which Nature ne'er decreed ;
And vicious ditties sings to please
Fell Dissipation's votaries.
Whane'er we reputation lose,
Fair Chastity's transparent gloss !
Redemption seenil kens the name ;
But a's black misery, and shame.

Frae joyous tavern, reelin drunk,
Wi' fiery phiz, and een half sunk,
Behold the bruiser, fae to a'
That in the reek o' gardies fa' !
Close by his side, a feckless race
O' macaronies shaw their face,
And think, they're free frae skaith or harm,
While pith befriend's their leader's arm :
Yet fearfu' aften o' their maught,
They quit the glory o' the faught
To this same warrior wha led
Thae heroes to bright Honour's bed ;

And aft the hack o' honour shines
In bruiser's face wi' broken lines.
O' them sad tales he tells anon,
Whan ramble and whan fighting's done :
And, like Hectorian, ne'er impairs
The brag and glory o' his sairs.

Whan feet in dirty gutters plash
And fock to wale their fitstaps fash ;
At night, the macaroni drunk,
In pools and gutters aft-times sunk :
Heh ! what a fright he now appears,
Whan he his corpse dejected rears !
Look at that head, and think if there
The pomet slaister'd up his hair !
The cheeks observe :—Where now cou'd shine
The scancin glories o' carmine ?
Ah, legs ! in vain the silk-worm there
Display'd to view her eident care :
For stink, instead of perfumes, grow,
And clarty odours fragrant flow.

Now, some to porter, some to punch—
Some to their wife,—and some their wench,—
Retire ;—while noisy ten-hour's drum
Gars a' your trades gae danderin home.
Now, mony a club, jocose and free,
Gie a' to merriment and glee :

Wi' sang, and glass, they fley the pow'r
O' Care, that wad harass the hour :
For wine and Bacchus still bear down
Our thrawart fortune's wildest frown ;
It maks you stark, and bauld, and brave,
Even whan descendin to the grave.

Now, some in Pandemonium's * shade,
Resume the gormandizin trade ;
Whare eager looks, and glancin een
Forespeak a heart and stamack keen.
Gang on, my lads ! it's lang sinsyne
We kent auld Epicurus' line.
Save you, the board wad cease to rise,
Bedight wi' daintiths to the skies ;
And salamanders cease to swill
The comforts o' a burning gill.

But chief, o' Cape ! * we crave thy aid,
To get our cares and poortith laid.
Sincerity, and genius true,
Of knights have ever been the due.
Mirth, music, porter deepest dyed,
Are never here to worth denied ;
And Health, o' happiness the queen,
Blinks bonny, wi' her smile serene.

* Pandemonium and the Cape were two social Clubs.

Tho' joy maist part Auld Reikie owns,
Eftsoons she kens sad sorrow's frowns.
What groupe is yon sae dismal, grim,
Wi' horrid aspect, cleedin dim?
Says Death, " they're mine ; a dowie crew:
" To me they'll shortly pay their last adieu."

How come mankind, whan lackin woe,
In Saulie's face their hearts to show ;
As if they were a clock, to tell
That grief in them had rung her bell?
Then, what is man? why a' this phrase?
Life's spunk decay'd nae mair can blaze.
Let sober grief alane declare
Our fond anxiety and care:
Nor let the undertakers be
The only waefu' friends we see.

Come on, my Muse! and then rehearse
The gloomiest theme in a' your verse.
In mornin, whan ane keeks about,
Fu' blithe, and free frae ail, nae doubt,
He lippens not to be misled
Amang the regions o' the dead:
But, straight, a painted corpse he sees,
Lang streekit 'neath its canopies.
Soon, soon will this his mirth control,
And send damnation to his soul.

Or whan the dead-deal, (awfu' shape!)
Maks frighted mankind girn and gape,
Reflection then his reason sours ;
For the niest dead-deal may be ours.
Whan Sybil led the Trojan down
To haggard Pluto's dreary town,
Shapes waur than thae, I freely ween,
Cou'd never meet the soldier's een.

If kail sae green, or herbs, delight,
Edina's street attracts the sight.
Not Covent-Garden, clad sae braw,
Mair fouth o' herbs can eithly shaw :
For mony a yard is here sair sought,
That kail and cabbage may be bought,
And healthfu' sallad, to regale,
Whan pamper'd wi' a heavy meal.
Glowr up the street in Simmer morn,
The birks sae green, and sweet brier thorn,
Wi' spraingit flow'rs that scent the gale,
Ca' far awa the mornin smell,
(Wi' which our ladies' flow'rpat's fill'd),
And every noxious vapour kill'd.
O Nature! canty, blithe, and free,
Whare is there keekin-glass like thee ?
Is there on earth that can compare
Wi' Mary's shape, and Mary's air,

Save the empurpled speck, that grows
In the saft faulds o' yonder rose?
How bonny seems the virgin breast,
Whan by the lilies here carest,
And leaves the mind in doubt to tell
Which maist in sweets and hue excel!

Gillespie's snuff shou'd prime the nose
O' her that to the market goes,
If she wad like to shun the smells
That float around frae market cells;
Whare wames o' painches' sav'ry scent
To nostrils gie great discontent.
Now, wha in Albion cou'd expect
O' cleanliness sic great neglect?
Nae Hottentot, that daily lairs
'Mang tripe, and ither clarty wares,
Hath ever yet conceiv'd, or seen,
Beyond the Line, sic scenes unclean.

On Sunday, here, an alter'd scene
O' men and manners meets our een.
Ane wad maist trow, some people chose
To change their faces wi' their clothes,
And fain wad gar ilk neebour think
They thirst for goodness, as for drink.
But there's an unco dearth o' grace,
That has nae mansion but the face,

And never can obtain a part
In benmost corner o' the heart.
Why shou'd religion mak us sad,
If good frae Virtue's to be had ?
Na : rather gleefu' turn you face ;
Forsake hypocrisy, grimace ;
And never hae it understood,
You fleg mankind frae being good.

In afternoon, a' brawly buskit,
The joes and lasses loe to frisk it.
Some tak a great delight to place
The modest bon-grace owre the face ;
Tho' you may see, if so inclin'd,
The turnin o' the leg behind.
Now, Comely-Garden, and the Park,
Refresh them, after forenoon's wark :
Newhaven, Leith, or Canonmills,
Supply them in their Sunday's gills ;
Whare writers aften spend their pence,
To stock their heads wi' drink and sense.

While dandering cits delight to stray
To Castlehill or public way,
Whare they nae other purpose mean,
Than that fool cause o' being seen ;
Let me to Arthur's Seat pursue,
Whare bonny pastures meet the view ;

And mony a wild-lorn scene accrues,
Befitting Willie Shakespeare's Muse.
If Fancy there wad join the thrang,
The desert rocks and hills amang,
To echoes we should lilt and play,
And gie to mirth the live-lang day.
   Or shou'd some canker'd biting shower
The day and a' her sweets deflower,
To Holyroodhouse let me stray,
And gie to musing a' the day;
Lamenting what auld Scotland knew,
Bien days for ever frae her view.
O Hamilton, for shame! the Muse
Wad pay to thee her couthy vows,
Gin ye wad tent the humble strain,
And gie's our dignity again:
For, oh, wae's me! the thistle springs
In domicil o' ancient kings,
Without a patriot to regret
Our palace, and our ancient state.

   Bless'd place! whare debtors daily run,
To rid themsels frae jail and dun.
Here, tho' sequester'd frae the din
That rings Auld Reikie's wa's within:
Yet they may tread the sunny braes,
And bruik Apollo's cheerie rays:
Glowr frae St Anthon's grassy height,
Owre vales in Simmer claes bedight;

Nor ever hing their head, I ween,
Wi' jealous fear o' being seen.
May I, whanever duns come nigh,
And shake my garret wi' their cry,
Scour here, wi' haste, protection get,
To screen mysel frae them and debt;
To breathe the bliss o' open sky,
And Simon Fraser's * bolts defy.

Now, gin a loun shou'd hae his claes
In threadbare autumn o' their days,
St Mary, broker's guardian saunt,
Will satisfy ilk ail and want;
For mony a hungry writer there
Dives down at night, wi' cleedin bare,
And quickly rises to the view
A gentleman perfyte, and new.
Ye rich fouk! look na wi' disdain
Upo' this ancient brokage lane,
For naked poets are supplied
Wi' what you to their wants denied.

Peace to thy shade, thou wale o' men,
Drummond! relief to poortith's pain.
To thee the greatest bliss we owe,
And tribute's tear shall gratefu' flow.

* Then keeper of the Tolbooth.

The sick are cured, the hungry fed,
And dreams o' comfort tend their bed.
As lang as Forth weets Lothian's shore;
As lang's on Fife her billows roar;
Sae lang shall ilk whase country's dear,
To thy remembrance gie a tear.
By thee, Auld Reikie thrave and grew,
Delightfu' to her childer's view.
Nae mair shall Glasgow striplings threap
Their city's beauty, and its shape,
While our new city spreads around
Her bonny wings on fairy ground.

But, Provosts now, that ne'er afford
The sma'est dignity to lord,
Ne'er care tho' every scheme gae wild
That Drummond's sacred hand has cull'd.
The spacious brig * neglected lies,
Tho' plagued wi' pamphlets, dunn'd wi' cries.
They heed not, tho' Destruction come
To gulp us in her gaunting womb.
Oh, shame! that safety canna claim
Protection from a Provost's name;
But hidden danger lies behind,
To torture, and to fleg the mind.

* An allusion to the state of the North Bridge after its fall.

I may as weel bid Arthur's Seat
To Berwick-Law mak gleg retreat,
As think that either will or art
Shall get the gate to win their heart:
For politics are a' their mark,
Bribes latent, and corruption dark.
If they can eithly turn the pence,
Wi' city's good they will dispense;
Nor care tho' a' her sons were lair'd
Ten fathom i' the auld kirkyard.

To sing yet meikle does remain,
Undecent for a modest strain;
And, since the poet's daily bread is
The favour o' the Muse, or ladies,
He downa like to gie offence
To Delicacy's tender sense;
Therefore, the stews remain unsung,
And bawds in silence drap their tongue.

Reikie, fareweel! I ne'er cou'd part
Wi' thee, but wi' a dowie heart.
Aft frae the Fifan coast I've seen
Thee towering on thy summit green.
So glowr the saints whan first is given
A favourite keek o' glore and heaven.
On earth nae mair they bend their een,
But quick assume angelic mien;

So I on Fife wad glowr no more,
But gallop'd to Edina's shore.

HAME CONTENT,

A SATIRE.

To all whom it may concern.

SOME fouk, like bees, fu' glegly rin
To bykes bang'd fu' o' strife and din,
And thieve and huddle crumb by crumb,
Till they hae scrap'd the dautit plumb,
Then craw fu' crously o' their wark,
Tell o'er their turners mark by mark,
Yet darena think to lowse the pose
To aid their neebours' ails and woes.

Gif gowd can fetter thus the heart,
And gar us act sae base a part;
Shall man, a niggard, near-gaun elf!
Rin to the tether's end for pelf;

Learn ilka cunzied scoundrel's trick,
Whan a's done sell his saul to Nick :
I trow they've cost the purchase dear,
That gang sic lengths for warldly gear.

Now, when the Dog-day heats begin
To birsle and to peel the skin,
May I lie streekit at my ease,
Beneath the cauler shady trees,
(Far frae the din o' borrows town),
Whare water plays the haughs bedown ;
To jouk the Simmer's rigour there,
And breathe a while the cauler air,
'Mang herds, and honest cottar fouk,
That till the farm, and feed the flock ;
Careless o' mair, wha never fash
To lade their kists wi' useless cash,
But thank the gods for what they've sent,
O' health eneugh, and blithe content,
And pith, that helps them to stravaig
Owre ilka cleugh, and ilka craig ;
Unkend to a' the weary granes
That aft arise frae gentler banes,
On easy-chair that pamper'd lie,
Wi' banefu' viands gustit high ;
And turn, and fauld their weary clay,
To rax and gaunt the live-lang day.

Ye sages, tell! was man e'er made
To dree this hatefu' sluggard trade,
Steekit frae Nature's beauties a'
That daily on his presence ca',
At hame to girn, and whinge, and pine
For favourite dishes, favourite wine?
Come, then, shake aff thir sluggish ties,
And wi' the bird o' dawning rise!
On ilka bank the clouds hae spread
Wi' blobs o' dew a pearly bed.
Frae faulds nae mair the owsen rout,
But to the fattening clover lout,
Whare they may feed at heart's content,
Unyokit frae their Winter's stent.
Unyoke, then, man! and binna sweer
To ding a hole in ill-hain'd gear.
O think that Eild, wi' wylie fit,
Is wearing nearer, bit by bit!
Gin aince he claws you wi' his paw,
What's siller for? Fient hae't ava!
But gowden playfair, that may please
The second sharger till he dies.

　　Some daft chiel reads, and taks advice;
The chaise is yokit in a trice;
Awa drives he, like huntit deil,
And scarce tholes time to cool his wheel,
Till he's—Lord kens how far awa!
At Italy, or Well o' Spa;

Or to Montpelier's safter air :
For far aff fowls hae feathers fair.

    There rest him weel :—for eith can we
Spare mony glaikit gowks like he.
They'll tell whare Tiber's waters rise ;
What sea receives the drumly prize ;
That never wi' their feet hae met
The marches o' their ain estate.

    The Arno and the Tiber lang
Hae run fell clear in Roman sang ;
But, save the reverence of schools !
They're baith but lifeless dowie pools.
Dought they compare wi' bonny Tweed,
As clear as ony lammer-bead ?
Or, are their shores mair sweet and gay
Than Fortha's haughs, or banks o' Tay ?
Tho' there the herds can jink the showers
'Mang thrivin vines and myrtle bowers,
And blaw the reed to kittle strains,
While Echo's tongue commends their pains ;
Like ours, they canna warm the heart
Wi' simple, saft, bewitchin art.
On Leader haughs, and Yarrow braes,
Arcadian herds wad tine their lays,
To hear the mair melodious sounds,
That live on our poetic grounds.

Come, Fancy! come, and let us tread
The Simmer's flowery velvet bed,
And a' your springs delightfu' lowse
On Tweeda's banks, or Cowdenknowes;
That, taen wi' thy enchantin sang,
Our Scottish lads may round ye thrang:
Sae pleas'd, they'll never fash again
To court you on Italian plain.
Soon will they guess, ye only wear
The simple garb o' Nature here;
Mair comely far, and fair to sight,
Whan in her easy cleedin dight,
Than, in disguise, ye was before
On Tiber's, or on Arno's shore.

O Bangour*! now the hills and dales
Nae mair gie back thy tender tales.
The birks on Yarrow now deplore,
Thy mournfu' Muse has left the shore.
Near what bright burn, or crystal spring,
Did you your winsome whistle hing?
The Muse shall there, wi' watery ee,
Gie the dunk swaird a tear for thee;
And Yarrow's genius, dowie dame!
Shall there forget her blude-stain'd stream,
On thy sad grave to seek repose,
Who mourn'd her fate, condol'd her woes.

* Mr Hamilton of Bangour.

THE

VANITY OF HUMAN WISHES.

An ELEGY *on the untimely Death of a* SCOTS POET.

BY MR JOHN TAIT.

Quis desiderio sit pudor, aut modus
Tam cari capitis? Præcipe lugubres
Cantus, Melpomene, cui liquidam pater
Vocem cum cithara dedit.

                                        HOR.

DARK was the night, and silence reigned o'er
    all ;
  No mirthful sounds urged on the lingering
    hour :
The sheeted ghost stalked thro' the stately hall ;
  And every breast confessed chill Horror's
    power.

Slumbering I lay : I mused on human hopes :
   " Vain, vain," I cried, " are all the hopes
      " we form !
" When Winter comes, the sweetest floweret
      " drops ;
   " And oaks themselves must bend before the
      " storm."

While thus I spake, a voice assailed my ear :
   'Twas sad ;—'twas slow ; it filled my mind
     with dread !
" Forbear," it cried ;—thy moral lays forbear :
   " Or change the strain, for FERGUSSON is
     " dead !

" Have we not seen him sporting on these
      " plains ?
   " Have we not heard him strike the MUSE's
      " lyre ?
" Have we not felt the magic of his strains,
   " Which often glow'd with Fancy's warmest
      " fire ?

" Have we not hop'd these strains would long
      " be heard ?
   " Have we not told how oft they touched the
      " soul ?

" And has not Scotia said, her youthful Bard
 " Might spread her fame even to the distant
  " pole ?

" But vain, alas ! are all the hopes we raised ;
 " Death strikes the blow—they sink—their
  " reign is o'er ;
" And these sweet songs, which we so oft have
 " praised—
 " These mirthful strains—shall now be heard
 " no more.

" This, this proclaims how vain are all the joys
 " Which we so ardently wish to attain ;
" Since ruthless Fate so oft, so soon destroys
 " The high-born hopes even of the Muses'
  " train."

I heard no more.—The cock, with clarion shrill,
 Loudly proclaimed th' approach of morning
  near—
The voice was gone—but yet I heard it still—
 For every note was echoed back by fear.

" Perhaps," I cried, " ere yonder rising sun
 " Shall sink his glories in the western wave ;
" Perhaps ere then my race too may be run,
 " And I myself laid in the silent grave.

" Oft then, O mortals! oft this dreadful truth
  " Should be proclaimed—for fate is in the
    " sound—
" That Genius, Learning, Health, and vigorous
  " Youth,
  " May, in one day, in Death's cold chains be
  " bound."

LINES,

Addressed to Mr R. FERGUSSON *on his Recovery
from severe Depression of Spirits,*

BY MR WOODS.

AND may thy friends the joyful news believe!
Dost thou to perfect sense and feeling live?
Has Pain, Despair, and Melancholy fled,
That shook their gloomy horrors round thy bed?
Has Reason chased the troubles of thy brain,
And fixed her native empire there again?

Has Health, first bliss! her saving arm in-
    clined,
And given thy body strength to suit thy mind?

Yes! it is true—again I see thee smile;
Again I view thee in the Muses' file,
With artless grace along their gardens move,
And twine wild wreaths as sportively you rove:
For all those friends, in thy affections joined,
By Sympathy, by Sentiment refined,
No words can justice to their joy afford,
To see a portion of *themselves* restored!
Even friends unknown—friends by thy merit
    earned,
Rejoice—while Dulness only's unconcerned:
Wit, Sense, and Fancy, all their powers display,
To celebrate thy second natal day.

So when some river, trembling with the
    storm,
Which sudden does its beauteous face deform,
Its wonted course no longer can maintain,
But bursts its banks and sweeps along the plain.
Soon as the angry whirlwinds cease to roar,
And sunny skies proclaim the tempest o'er,
No more on stranger shores the surges foam,
But creep in murmurs to their native home;

Untaught by art, their parent waters know,
And once more freely and unruffled flow*.

W.

* These verses were originally published in the Caledonian Mercury (Saturday, July 9th 1774), and are now annexed as a suitable accompaniment to the other Poetical tributes of respect for Fergusson.

F I N I S.

OLIVER & CO. PRINTERS, EDINBURGH.